Chatbots Strategy
Complete Self-Assessment

The guidance in this Self-Assessment is based on Chatbots Strategy best practices and standards in business process architecture, design and quality management. The guidance is also based on the professional judgment of the individual collaborators listed in the Acknowledgments.

Notice of rights

Trademarks

Table of Contents

About The Art of Service

The Art of Service, Business Process Architects since 2000, is dedicated to helping stakeholders achieve excellence.

Defining, designing, creating, and implementing a process to solve a stakeholders challenge or meet an objective is the most valuable role… In EVERY group, company, organization and department.

Unless you're talking a one-time, single-use project, there should be a process. Whether that process is managed and implemented by humans, AI, or a combination of the two, it needs to be designed by someone with a complex enough perspective to ask the right questions.

Someone capable of asking the right questions and step back and say, 'What are we really trying to accomplish here? And is there a different way to look at it?'

With The Art of Service's Standard Requirements Self-Assessments, we empower people who can do just that — whether their title is marketer, entrepreneur, manager, salesperson, consultant, Business Process Manager, executive assistant, IT Manager, CIO etc... —they are the people who rule the future. They are people who watch the process as it happens, and ask the right questions to make the process work better.

Contact us when you need any support with this Self-Assessment and any help with templates, blue-prints and examples of standard documents you might need:

http://theartofservice.com
service@theartofservice.com

Included Resources - how to access

Included with your purchase of the book is the Chatbots

Strategy Self-Assessment Spreadsheet Dashboard which contains all questions and Self-Assessment areas and auto-generates insights, graphs, and project RACI planning - all with examples to get you started right away.

How? Simply send an email to
access@theartofservice.com
with this books' title in the subject to get the Chatbots Strategy Self Assessment Tool right away.

You will receive the following contents with New and Updated specific criteria:

- The latest quick edition of the book in PDF

- The latest complete edition of the book in PDF, which criteria correspond to the criteria in...

- The Self-Assessment Excel Dashboard, and...

- Example pre-filled Self-Assessment Excel Dashboard to get familiar with results generation

- In-depth specific Checklists covering the topic

- Project management checklists and templates to assist with implementation

INCLUDES LIFETIME SELF ASSESSMENT UPDATES

Every self assessment comes with Lifetime Updates and Lifetime Free Updated Books. Lifetime Updates is an industry-first feature which allows you to receive verified self assessment updates, ensuring you always have the most accurate information at your fingertips.

Get it now- you will be glad you did - do it now, before you forget.

Send an email to **access@theartofservice.com** with this books' title in the subject to get the Chatbots Strategy Self Assessment Tool right away.

Purpose of this Self-Assessment

This Self-Assessment has been developed to improve understanding of the requirements and elements of Chatbots Strategy, based on best practices and standards in business process architecture, design and quality management.

It is designed to allow for a rapid Self-Assessment to determine how closely existing management practices and procedures correspond to the elements of the Self-Assessment.

The criteria of requirements and elements of Chatbots Strategy have been rephrased in the format of a Self-Assessment questionnaire, with a seven-criterion scoring system, as explained in this document.

In this format, even with limited background knowledge of Chatbots Strategy, a manager can quickly review existing operations to determine how they measure up to the standards. This in turn can serve as the starting point of a 'gap analysis' to identify management tools or system elements that might usefully be implemented in the organization to help improve overall performance.

How to use the Self-Assessment

On the following pages are a series of questions to identify to what extent your Chatbots Strategy initiative is complete in comparison to the requirements set in standards.

To facilitate answering the questions, there is a space in front of each question to enter a score on a scale of '1' to '5'.

1 Strongly Disagree

2 Disagree

3 Neutral

4 Agree

5 Strongly Agree

Read the question and rate it with the following in front of mind:

'In my belief, the answer to this question is clearly defined'.

There are two ways in which you can choose to interpret this statement;
1. how aware are you that the answer to the question is clearly defined
2. for more in-depth analysis you can choose to gather evidence and confirm the answer to the question. This obviously will take more time, most Self-Assessment users opt for the first way to interpret the question and dig deeper later on based on the outcome of the overall Self-Assessment.

A score of '1' would mean that the answer is not clear at all, where a '5' would mean the answer is crystal clear and defined. Leave emtpy when the question is not applicable or you don't want to answer it, you can skip it without affecting your score. Write your score in the space provided.

After you have responded to all the appropriate statements in each section, compute your average score for that section, using the formula provided, and round to the nearest tenth. Then transfer to the corresponding spoke in the Chatbots Strategy Scorecard on the second next page of the Self-Assessment.

Your completed Chatbots Strategy Scorecard will give you a clear presentation of which Chatbots Strategy areas need attention.

Chatbots Strategy
Scorecard Example

Example of how the finalized Scorecard can look like:

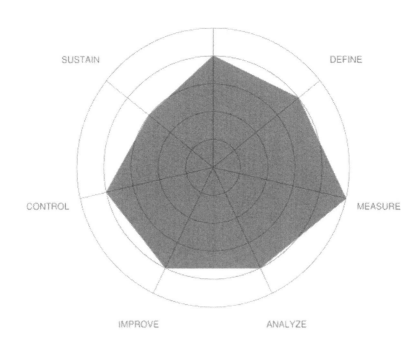

Chatbots Strategy Scorecard

Your Scores:

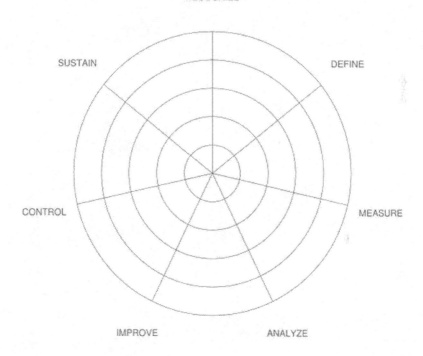

BEGINNING OF THE SELF-ASSESSMENT:

CRITERION #1: RECOGNIZE

INTENT: Be aware of the need for change. Recognize that there is an unfavorable variation, problem or symptom.

In my belief, the answer to this question is clearly defined:

5 Strongly Agree

4 Agree

3 Neutral

2 Disagree

1 Strongly Disagree

1. What are the timeframes required to resolve each of the issues/problems?
<--- Score

2. How do you recognize an chatbots strategy objection?
<--- Score

3. Are losses recognized in a timely manner?

<--- Score

4. Who needs budgets?
<--- Score

5. What are the chatbots strategy resources needed?
<--- Score

6. What is the extent or complexity of the chatbots strategy problem?
<--- Score

7. Whom do you really need or want to serve?
<--- Score

8. What chatbots strategy capabilities do you need?
<--- Score

9. Would you recognize a threat from the inside?
<--- Score

10. Are your goals realistic? Do you need to redefine your problem? Perhaps the problem has changed or maybe you have reached your goal and need to set a new one?
<--- Score

11. Who needs to know about chatbots strategy?
<--- Score

12. What needs to be done?
<--- Score

13. Are there any specific expectations or concerns about the chatbots strategy team, chatbots strategy itself?

<--- Score

14. Think about the people you identified for your chatbots strategy project and the project responsibilities you would assign to them, what kind of training do you think they would need to perform these responsibilities effectively?
<--- Score

15. What training and capacity building actions are needed to implement proposed reforms?
<--- Score

16. For your chatbots strategy project, identify and describe the business environment, is there more than one layer to the business environment?
<--- Score

17. Does chatbots strategy create potential expectations in other areas that need to be recognized and considered?
<--- Score

18. What resources or support might you need?
<--- Score

19. How can auditing be a preventative security measure?
<--- Score

20. Did you miss any major chatbots strategy issues?
<--- Score

21. What else needs to be measured?
<--- Score

22. What is the smallest subset of the problem you can usefully solve?
<--- Score

23. Are employees recognized for desired behaviors?
<--- Score

24. Why is this needed?
<--- Score

25. Which issues are too important to ignore?
<--- Score

26. How do you identify the kinds of information that you will need?
<--- Score

27. What problems are you facing and how do you consider chatbots strategy will circumvent those obstacles?
<--- Score

28. What do employees need in the short term?
<--- Score

29. Who needs what information?
<--- Score

30. What tools and technologies are needed for a custom chatbots strategy project?
<--- Score

31. How do you identify subcontractor relationships?
<--- Score

32. Are there any revenue recognition issues?

<--- Score

33. Do you know what you need to know about chatbots strategy?
<--- Score

34. What is the recognized need?
<--- Score

35. Which information does the chatbots strategy business case need to include?
<--- Score

36. What chatbots strategy coordination do you need?
<--- Score

37. What extra resources will you need?
<--- Score

38. Who should resolve the chatbots strategy issues?
<--- Score

39. What creative shifts do you need to take?
<--- Score

40. Does the problem have ethical dimensions?
<--- Score

41. Are there regulatory / compliance issues?
<--- Score

42. Which needs are not included or involved?
<--- Score

43. When a chatbots strategy manager recognizes a problem, what options are available?

<--- Score

44. How are training requirements identified?
<--- Score

45. What information do users need?
<--- Score

46. Do you need to avoid or amend any chatbots strategy activities?
<--- Score

47. How are you going to measure success?
<--- Score

48. What is the problem and/or vulnerability?
<--- Score

49. What chatbots strategy problem should be solved?
<--- Score

50. What needs to stay?
<--- Score

51. Who are your key stakeholders who need to sign off?
<--- Score

52. What is the problem or issue?
<--- Score

53. As a sponsor, customer or management, how important is it to meet goals, objectives?
<--- Score

54. What does chatbots strategy success mean to the

stakeholders?
<--- Score

55. How many trainings, in total, are needed?
<--- Score

56. What should be considered when identifying available resources, constraints, and deadlines?
<--- Score

57. What are the expected benefits of chatbots strategy to the stakeholder?
<--- Score

58. Do you have/need 24-hour access to key personnel?
<--- Score

59. What do you need to start doing?
<--- Score

60. Are there chatbots strategy problems defined?
<--- Score

61. What are your needs in relation to chatbots strategy skills, labor, equipment, and markets?
<--- Score

62. What vendors make products that address the chatbots strategy needs?
<--- Score

63. Are problem definition and motivation clearly presented?
<--- Score

64. Are controls defined to recognize and contain problems?
<--- Score

65. Do you recognize chatbots strategy achievements?
<--- Score

66. What situation(s) led to this chatbots strategy Self Assessment?
<--- Score

67. Looking at each person individually – does every one have the qualities which are needed to work in this group?
<--- Score

68. How does it fit into your organizational needs and tasks?
<--- Score

69. Where do you need to exercise leadership?
<--- Score

70. Is it needed?
<--- Score

71. Will new equipment/products be required to facilitate chatbots strategy delivery, for example is new software needed?
<--- Score

72. Will a response program recognize when a crisis occurs and provide some level of response?
<--- Score

73. To what extent would your organization benefit from being recognized as a award recipient?
<--- Score

74. How do you recognize an objection?
<--- Score

75. Where is training needed?
<--- Score

76. Does your organization need more chatbots strategy education?
<--- Score

77. Who else hopes to benefit from it?
<--- Score

78. What is the chatbots strategy problem definition? What do you need to resolve?
<--- Score

79. Can management personnel recognize the monetary benefit of chatbots strategy?
<--- Score

80. What chatbots strategy events should you attend?
<--- Score

81. What activities does the governance board need to consider?
<--- Score

82. Are employees recognized or rewarded for performance that demonstrates the highest levels of integrity?
<--- Score

83. Consider your own chatbots strategy project, what types of organizational problems do you think might be causing or affecting your problem, based on the work done so far?
<--- Score

84. Is the need for organizational change recognized?
<--- Score

85. Will it solve real problems?
<--- Score

86. Are you dealing with any of the same issues today as yesterday? What can you do about this?
<--- Score

87. Is the quality assurance team identified?
<--- Score

88. What would happen if chatbots strategy weren't done?
<--- Score

89. To what extent does each concerned units management team recognize chatbots strategy as an effective investment?
<--- Score

90. Who defines the rules in relation to any given issue?
<--- Score

91. How do you assess your chatbots strategy workforce capability and capacity needs, including skills, competencies, and staffing levels?

<--- Score

92. How much are sponsors, customers, partners, stakeholders involved in chatbots strategy? In other words, what are the risks, if chatbots strategy does not deliver successfully?
<--- Score

93. Do you need different information or graphics?
<--- Score

94. How are the chatbots strategy's objectives aligned to the group's overall stakeholder strategy?
<--- Score

95. Why the need?
<--- Score

96. What are the minority interests and what amount of minority interests can be recognized?
<--- Score

97. Who needs to know?
<--- Score

98. What are the clients issues and concerns?
<--- Score

99. What are the stakeholder objectives to be achieved with chatbots strategy?
<--- Score

100. What prevents you from making the changes you know will make you a more effective chatbots strategy leader?
<--- Score

101. How do you take a forward-looking perspective in identifying chatbots strategy research related to market response and models?
<--- Score

Add up total points for this section:
_____ = Total points for this section

Divided by: _____ (number of statements answered) = _____
Average score for this section

Transfer your score to the chatbots strategy Index at the beginning of the Self-Assessment.

CRITERION #2: DEFINE:

INTENT: Formulate the stakeholder problem. Define the problem, needs and objectives.

In my belief, the answer to this question is clearly defined:

5 Strongly Agree

4 Agree

3 Neutral

2 Disagree

1 Strongly Disagree

1. What is the scope?
<--- Score

2. Is the team equipped with available and reliable resources?
<--- Score

3. What critical content must be communicated – who, what, when, where, and how?

<--- Score

4. How do you manage scope?
<--- Score

5. Has a high-level 'as is' process map been completed, verified and validated?
<--- Score

6. What are the tasks and definitions?
<--- Score

7. What intelligence can you gather?
<--- Score

8. Is full participation by members in regularly held team meetings guaranteed?
<--- Score

9. Why are you doing chatbots strategy and what is the scope?
<--- Score

10. How will the chatbots strategy team and the group measure complete success of chatbots strategy?
<--- Score

11. Where can you gather more information?
<--- Score

12. What are the boundaries of the scope? What is in bounds and what is not? What is the start point? What is the stop point?
<--- Score

13. How have you defined all chatbots strategy requirements first?
<--- Score

14. Who approved the chatbots strategy scope?
<--- Score

15. Has everyone on the team, including the team leaders, been properly trained?
<--- Score

16. What baselines are required to be defined and managed?
<--- Score

17. Are accountability and ownership for chatbots strategy clearly defined?
<--- Score

18. What are the requirements for audit information?
<--- Score

19. What is in the scope and what is not in scope?
<--- Score

20. What scope do you want your strategy to cover?
<--- Score

21. Is there a critical path to deliver chatbots strategy results?
<--- Score

22. What is the worst case scenario?
<--- Score

23. What is the scope of the chatbots strategy effort?

<--- Score

24. Do you all define chatbots strategy in the same way?
<--- Score

25. How did the chatbots strategy manager receive input to the development of a chatbots strategy improvement plan and the estimated completion dates/times of each activity?
<--- Score

26. What system do you use for gathering chatbots strategy information?
<--- Score

27. When are meeting minutes sent out? Who is on the distribution list?
<--- Score

28. Is it clearly defined in and to your organization what you do?
<--- Score

29. Are roles and responsibilities formally defined?
<--- Score

30. Are resources adequate for the scope?
<--- Score

31. How do you build the right business case?
<--- Score

32. Is there a completed, verified, and validated high-level 'as is' (not 'should be' or 'could be') stakeholder process map?

<--- Score

33. What specifically is the problem? Where does it occur? When does it occur? What is its extent?
<--- Score

34. Is there regularly 100% attendance at the team meetings? If not, have appointed substitutes attended to preserve cross-functionality and full representation?
<--- Score

35. Are improvement team members fully trained on chatbots strategy?
<--- Score

36. Have all of the relationships been defined properly?
<--- Score

37. Is chatbots strategy currently on schedule according to the plan?
<--- Score

38. Are different versions of process maps needed to account for the different types of inputs?
<--- Score

39. What constraints exist that might impact the team?
<--- Score

40. Are approval levels defined for contracts and supplements to contracts?
<--- Score

41. What are (control) requirements for chatbots strategy Information?
<--- Score

42. Do you have organizational privacy requirements?
<--- Score

43. What are the chatbots strategy use cases?
<--- Score

44. Who defines (or who defined) the rules and roles?
<--- Score

45. What is a worst-case scenario for losses?
<--- Score

46. Are customer(s) identified and segmented according to their different needs and requirements?
<--- Score

47. Has the chatbots strategy work been fairly and/or equitably divided and delegated among team members who are qualified and capable to perform the work? Has everyone contributed?
<--- Score

48. Is the team adequately staffed with the desired cross-functionality? If not, what additional resources are available to the team?
<--- Score

49. What customer feedback methods were used to solicit their input?
<--- Score

50. Is special chatbots strategy user knowledge

required?
<--- Score

51. When is the estimated completion date?
<--- Score

52. What are the Roles and Responsibilities for each team member and its leadership? Where is this documented?
<--- Score

53. Are the chatbots strategy requirements testable?
<--- Score

54. In what way can you redefine the criteria of choice clients have in your category in your favor?
<--- Score

55. Have the customer needs been translated into specific, measurable requirements? How?
<--- Score

56. Is the scope of chatbots strategy defined?
<--- Score

57. Is chatbots strategy linked to key stakeholder goals and objectives?
<--- Score

58. How does the chatbots strategy manager ensure against scope creep?
<--- Score

59. Is there a clear chatbots strategy case definition?
<--- Score

60. Is chatbots strategy required?
<--- Score

61. What is in scope?
<--- Score

62. Will team members perform chatbots strategy work when assigned and in a timely fashion?
<--- Score

63. Is the team formed and are team leaders (Coaches and Management Leads) assigned?
<--- Score

64. How often are the team meetings?
<--- Score

65. How was the 'as is' process map developed, reviewed, verified and validated?
<--- Score

66. How do you think the partners involved in chatbots strategy would have defined success?
<--- Score

67. What information do you gather?
<--- Score

68. What happens if chatbots strategy's scope changes?
<--- Score

69. How will variation in the actual durations of each activity be dealt with to ensure that the expected chatbots strategy results are met?
<--- Score

70. Has a team charter been developed and communicated?
<--- Score

71. What is the definition of success?
<--- Score

72. Are there any constraints known that bear on the ability to perform chatbots strategy work? How is the team addressing them?
<--- Score

73. What scope to assess?
<--- Score

74. How is the team tracking and documenting its work?
<--- Score

75. Is the team sponsored by a champion or stakeholder leader?
<--- Score

76. Are audit criteria, scope, frequency and methods defined?
<--- Score

77. Is data collected and displayed to better understand customer(s) critical needs and requirements.
<--- Score

78. How do you manage unclear chatbots strategy requirements?
<--- Score

79. What key stakeholder process output measure(s) does chatbots strategy leverage and how?
<--- Score

80. How do you keep key subject matter experts in the loop?
<--- Score

81. What chatbots strategy requirements should be gathered?
<--- Score

82. What are the record-keeping requirements of chatbots strategy activities?
<--- Score

83. Have all basic functions of chatbots strategy been defined?
<--- Score

84. Has the direction changed at all during the course of chatbots strategy? If so, when did it change and why?
<--- Score

85. What was the context?
<--- Score

86. Has the improvement team collected the 'voice of the customer' (obtained feedback – qualitative and quantitative)?
<--- Score

87. What knowledge or experience is required?
<--- Score

88. Has anyone else (internal or external to the group) attempted to solve this problem or a similar one before? If so, what knowledge can be leveraged from these previous efforts?
<--- Score

89. What is out of scope?
<--- Score

90. Is there a completed SIPOC representation, describing the Suppliers, Inputs, Process, Outputs, and Customers?
<--- Score

91. How do you gather requirements?
<--- Score

92. Do the problem and goal statements meet the SMART criteria (specific, measurable, attainable, relevant, and time-bound)?
<--- Score

93. Are the chatbots strategy requirements complete?
<--- Score

94. How would you define the culture at your organization, how susceptible is it to chatbots strategy changes?
<--- Score

95. Will team members regularly document their chatbots strategy work?
<--- Score

96. Is the improvement team aware of the different

versions of a process: what they think it is vs. what it actually is vs. what it should be vs. what it could be?
<--- Score

97. Is the current 'as is' process being followed? If not, what are the discrepancies?
<--- Score

98. What sort of initial information to gather?
<--- Score

99. Is there any additional chatbots strategy definition of success?
<--- Score

100. If substitutes have been appointed, have they been briefed on the chatbots strategy goals and received regular communications as to the progress to date?
<--- Score

101. How do you hand over chatbots strategy context?
<--- Score

102. What is the scope of the chatbots strategy work?
<--- Score

103. Is there a chatbots strategy management charter, including stakeholder case, problem and goal statements, scope, milestones, roles and responsibilities, communication plan?
<--- Score

104. When is/was the chatbots strategy start date?
<--- Score

105. Has/have the customer(s) been identified?
<--- Score

106. What are the compelling stakeholder reasons for embarking on chatbots strategy?
<--- Score

107. Who is gathering chatbots strategy information?
<--- Score

108. What is the scope of chatbots strategy?
<--- Score

109. Is the chatbots strategy scope manageable?
<--- Score

110. How do you manage changes in chatbots strategy requirements?
<--- Score

111. What are the chatbots strategy tasks and definitions?
<--- Score

112. How do you gather the stories?
<--- Score

113. Who are the chatbots strategy improvement team members, including Management Leads and Coaches?
<--- Score

114. Have specific policy objectives been defined?
<--- Score

115. Is the chatbots strategy scope complete and appropriately sized?
<--- Score

116. How do you gather chatbots strategy requirements?
<--- Score

117. What gets examined?
<--- Score

118. Do you have a chatbots strategy success story or case study ready to tell and share?
<--- Score

119. Does the team have regular meetings?
<--- Score

120. What are the rough order estimates on cost savings/opportunities that chatbots strategy brings?
<--- Score

121. What would be the goal or target for a chatbots strategy's improvement team?
<--- Score

122. Will a chatbots strategy production readiness review be required?
<--- Score

123. What are the dynamics of the communication plan?
<--- Score

124. What is out-of-scope initially?
<--- Score

125. Is the work to date meeting requirements?
<--- Score

126. How would you define chatbots strategy
leadership?
<--- Score

127. What sources do you use to gather information
for a chatbots strategy study?
<--- Score

128. What defines best in class?
<--- Score

129. How do you catch chatbots strategy definition
inconsistencies?
<--- Score

130. Has a project plan, Gantt chart, or similar been
developed/completed?
<--- Score

131. Are task requirements clearly defined?
<--- Score

132. What chatbots strategy services do you require?
<--- Score

133. Does the scope remain the same?
<--- Score

134. Are there different segments of customers?
<--- Score

135. What is the definition of chatbots strategy

excellence?
<--- Score

136. How and when will the baselines be defined?
<--- Score

137. Who is gathering information?
<--- Score

138. What is the context?
<--- Score

Add up total points for this section:
_____ = Total points for this section

Divided by: _____ (number of
statements answered) = _____
Average score for this section

Transfer your score to the chatbots
strategy Index at the beginning of the
Self-Assessment.

CRITERION #3: MEASURE:

INTENT: Gather the correct data.
Measure the current performance and
evolution of the situation.

In my belief, the answer to this
question is clearly defined:

5 Strongly Agree

4 Agree

3 Neutral

2 Disagree

1 Strongly Disagree

1. What does your operating model cost?
<--- Score

2. What is the cost of rework?
<--- Score

3. Will chatbots strategy have an impact on current
business continuity, disaster recovery processes and/
or infrastructure?

<--- Score

4. Where is it measured?
<--- Score

5. How will your organization measure success?
<--- Score

6. How do you measure success?
<--- Score

7. When a disaster occurs, who gets priority?
<--- Score

8. How do you verify performance?
<--- Score

9. What relevant entities could be measured?
<--- Score

10. Is it possible to estimate the impact of unanticipated complexity such as wrong or failed assumptions, feedback, etcetera on proposed reforms?
<--- Score

11. How can you measure the performance?
<--- Score

12. What is the cause of any chatbots strategy gaps?
<--- Score

13. How will effects be measured?
<--- Score

14. Do you aggressively reward and promote the

people who have the biggest impact on creating excellent chatbots strategy services/products?
<--- Score

15. What happens if cost savings do not materialize?
<--- Score

16. Who should receive measurement reports?
<--- Score

17. Have design-to-cost goals been established?
<--- Score

18. What are the costs of reform?
<--- Score

19. What could cause delays in the schedule?
<--- Score

20. How do you verify and validate the chatbots strategy data?
<--- Score

21. How do you measure variability?
<--- Score

22. What are the uncertainties surrounding estimates of impact?
<--- Score

23. How long to keep data and how to manage retention costs?
<--- Score

24. How frequently do you verify your chatbots strategy strategy?

<--- Score

25. What are your primary costs, revenues, assets?
<--- Score

26. What can be used to verify compliance?
<--- Score

27. Are there measurements based on task performance?
<--- Score

28. When should you bother with diagrams?
<--- Score

29. How will measures be used to manage and adapt?
<--- Score

30. What users will be impacted?
<--- Score

31. How do you aggregate measures across priorities?
<--- Score

32. What does a Test Case verify?
<--- Score

33. Are indirect costs charged to the chatbots strategy program?
<--- Score

34. How do you control the overall costs of your work processes?
<--- Score

35. What are the chatbots strategy key cost drivers?

<--- Score

36. What does verifying compliance entail?
<--- Score

37. What is the total fixed cost?
<--- Score

38. At what cost?
<--- Score

39. How can you reduce costs?
<--- Score

40. How will you measure your chatbots strategy effectiveness?
<--- Score

41. What causes mismanagement?
<--- Score

42. What do you measure and why?
<--- Score

43. How is performance measured?
<--- Score

44. How can you measure chatbots strategy in a systematic way?
<--- Score

45. What are the strategic priorities for this year?
<--- Score

46. How are measurements made?
<--- Score

47. What measurements are being captured?
<--- Score

48. Do you have any cost chatbots strategy limitation requirements?
<--- Score

49. Do you have a flow diagram of what happens?
<--- Score

50. What does losing customers cost your organization?
<--- Score

51. Where can you go to verify the info?
<--- Score

52. What is an unallowable cost?
<--- Score

53. What are hidden chatbots strategy quality costs?
<--- Score

54. What are the chatbots strategy investment costs?
<--- Score

55. How to cause the change?
<--- Score

56. What disadvantage does this cause for the user?
<--- Score

57. Is there an opportunity to verify requirements?
<--- Score

58. How will costs be allocated?
<--- Score

59. What methods are feasible and acceptable to estimate the impact of reforms?
<--- Score

60. Are you taking your company in the direction of better and revenue or cheaper and cost?
<--- Score

61. Does a chatbots strategy quantification method exist?
<--- Score

62. How can you manage cost down?
<--- Score

63. Who is involved in verifying compliance?
<--- Score

64. Are chatbots strategy vulnerabilities categorized and prioritized?
<--- Score

65. How do you quantify and qualify impacts?
<--- Score

66. What details are required of the chatbots strategy cost structure?
<--- Score

67. How do you prevent mis-estimating cost?
<--- Score

68. How are costs allocated?

<--- Score

69. Did you tackle the cause or the symptom?
<--- Score

70. What are the costs of delaying chatbots strategy action?
<--- Score

71. How do you verify if chatbots strategy is built right?
<--- Score

72. How do you measure lifecycle phases?
<--- Score

73. How do your measurements capture actionable chatbots strategy information for use in exceeding your customers expectations and securing your customers engagement?
<--- Score

74. When are costs are incurred?
<--- Score

75. What causes innovation to fail or succeed in your organization?
<--- Score

76. Are there any easy-to-implement alternatives to chatbots strategy? Sometimes other solutions are available that do not require the cost implications of a full-blown project?
<--- Score

77. Which costs should be taken into account?

<--- Score

78. What evidence is there and what is measured?
<--- Score

79. Are the units of measure consistent?
<--- Score

80. What are the costs?
<--- Score

81. How do you stay flexible and focused to recognize larger chatbots strategy results?
<--- Score

82. Why a chatbots strategy focus?
<--- Score

83. Is the cost worth the chatbots strategy effort ?
<--- Score

84. Are there competing chatbots strategy priorities?
<--- Score

85. How is the value delivered by chatbots strategy being measured?
<--- Score

86. What is the total cost related to deploying chatbots strategy, including any consulting or professional services?
<--- Score

87. What is the root cause(s) of the problem?
<--- Score

88. Do the benefits outweigh the costs?
<--- Score

89. What is your decision requirements diagram?
<--- Score

90. What are the types and number of measures to use?
<--- Score

91. How do you verify the authenticity of the data and information used?
<--- Score

92. What could cause you to change course?
<--- Score

93. Where is the cost?
<--- Score

94. Why do you expend time and effort to implement measurement, for whom?
<--- Score

95. Do you have an issue in getting priority?
<--- Score

96. What is the chatbots strategy business impact?
<--- Score

97. What are your operating costs?
<--- Score

98. What potential environmental factors impact the chatbots strategy effort?
<--- Score

99. How do you verify the chatbots strategy requirements quality?
<--- Score

100. Are you aware of what could cause a problem?
<--- Score

101. Does management have the right priorities among projects?
<--- Score

102. How can a chatbots strategy test verify your ideas or assumptions?
<--- Score

103. Are missed chatbots strategy opportunities costing your organization money?
<--- Score

104. Are the measurements objective?
<--- Score

105. What harm might be caused?
<--- Score

106. How is progress measured?
<--- Score

107. What measurements are possible, practicable and meaningful?
<--- Score

108. Have you included everything in your chatbots strategy cost models?
<--- Score

109. What are your customers expectations and measures?
<--- Score

110. What drives O&M cost?
<--- Score

111. How do you verify and develop ideas and innovations?
<--- Score

112. Are you able to realize any cost savings?
<--- Score

113. How much does it cost?
<--- Score

114. How do you measure efficient delivery of chatbots strategy services?
<--- Score

115. Do you effectively measure and reward individual and team performance?
<--- Score

116. How will you measure success?
<--- Score

117. What causes extra work or rework?
<--- Score

118. What are the estimated costs of proposed changes?
<--- Score

119. What are the costs and benefits?
<--- Score

120. How frequently do you track chatbots strategy measures?
<--- Score

121. Who pays the cost?
<--- Score

122. Is a follow-up focused external chatbots strategy review required?
<--- Score

123. Have you made assumptions about the shape of the future, particularly its impact on your customers and competitors?
<--- Score

124. What tests verify requirements?
<--- Score

125. How will the chatbots strategy data be analyzed?
<--- Score

126. Does the chatbots strategy task fit the client's priorities?
<--- Score

127. What would be a real cause for concern?
<--- Score

128. How sensitive must the chatbots strategy strategy be to cost?
<--- Score

129. How do you verify chatbots strategy completeness and accuracy?
<--- Score

130. Has a cost center been established?
<--- Score

131. Do you verify that corrective actions were taken?
<--- Score

132. What would it cost to replace your technology?
<--- Score

133. Are actual costs in line with budgeted costs?
<--- Score

134. What is measured? Why?
<--- Score

135. Which measures and indicators matter?
<--- Score

136. What are the current costs of the chatbots strategy process?
<--- Score

137. How are you verifying it?
<--- Score

138. How do you focus on what is right -not who is right?
<--- Score

139. Why do the measurements/indicators matter?
<--- Score

140. How will success or failure be measured?
<--- Score

141. What are your key chatbots strategy organizational performance measures, including key short and longer-term financial measures?
<--- Score

Add up total points for this section:
_ _ _ _ _ = Total points for this section

Divided by: _ _ _ _ _ _ (number of statements answered) = _ _ _ _ _ _
Average score for this section

Transfer your score to the chatbots strategy Index at the beginning of the Self-Assessment.

CRITERION #4: ANALYZE:

INTENT: Analyze causes, assumptions and hypotheses.

In my belief, the answer to this question is clearly defined:

5 Strongly Agree

4 Agree

3 Neutral

2 Disagree

1 Strongly Disagree

1. What did the team gain from developing a sub-process map?
<--- Score

2. How is chatbots strategy data gathered?
<--- Score

3. What are the revised rough estimates of the financial savings/opportunity for chatbots strategy improvements?

<--- Score

4. Identify an operational issue in your organization, for example, could a particular task be done more quickly or more efficiently by chatbots strategy?
<--- Score

5. What quality tools were used to get through the analyze phase?
<--- Score

6. Are chatbots strategy changes recognized early enough to be approved through the regular process?
<--- Score

7. Were any designed experiments used to generate additional insight into the data analysis?
<--- Score

8. What internal processes need improvement?
<--- Score

9. What are your outputs?
<--- Score

10. Who is involved in the management review process?
<--- Score

11. What process should you select for improvement?
<--- Score

12. How are outputs preserved and protected?
<--- Score

13. What qualifications are necessary?

<--- Score

14. Who gets your output?
<--- Score

15. Is there any way to speed up the process?
<--- Score

16. Are gaps between current performance and the goal performance identified?
<--- Score

17. Where is chatbots strategy data gathered?
<--- Score

18. How often will data be collected for measures?
<--- Score

19. Think about some of the processes you undertake within your organization, which do you own?
<--- Score

20. What were the crucial 'moments of truth' on the process map?
<--- Score

21. How do you ensure that the chatbots strategy opportunity is realistic?
<--- Score

22. Record-keeping requirements flow from the records needed as inputs, outputs, controls and for transformation of a chatbots strategy process, are the records needed as inputs to the chatbots strategy process available?
<--- Score

23. What is the oversight process?
<--- Score

24. Do your leaders quickly bounce back from setbacks?
<--- Score

25. Have any additional benefits been identified that will result from closing all or most of the gaps?
<--- Score

26. Was a cause-and-effect diagram used to explore the different types of causes (or sources of variation)?
<--- Score

27. What are the processes for audit reporting and management?
<--- Score

28. What resources go in to get the desired output?
<--- Score

29. How do you implement and manage your work processes to ensure that they meet design requirements?
<--- Score

30. Is there an established change management process?
<--- Score

31. Are you missing chatbots strategy opportunities?
<--- Score

32. What are the chatbots strategy design outputs?

<--- Score

33. What are your best practices for minimizing chatbots strategy project risk, while demonstrating incremental value and quick wins throughout the chatbots strategy project lifecycle?
<--- Score

34. Do your employees have the opportunity to do what they do best everyday?
<--- Score

35. Think about the functions involved in your chatbots strategy project, what processes flow from these functions?
<--- Score

36. Did any value-added analysis or 'lean thinking' take place to identify some of the gaps shown on the 'as is' process map?
<--- Score

37. What is your organizations system for selecting qualified vendors?
<--- Score

38. Did any additional data need to be collected?
<--- Score

39. Do you have the authority to produce the output?
<--- Score

40. What systems/processes must you excel at?
<--- Score

41. How is the way you as the leader think and process

information affecting your organizational culture?
<--- Score

42. A compounding model resolution with available relevant data can often provide insight towards a solution methodology; which chatbots strategy models, tools and techniques are necessary?
<--- Score

43. How do you measure the operational performance of your key work systems and processes, including productivity, cycle time, and other appropriate measures of process effectiveness, efficiency, and innovation?
<--- Score

44. How will the chatbots strategy data be captured?
<--- Score

45. Has an output goal been set?
<--- Score

46. Who will facilitate the team and process?
<--- Score

47. Is the final output clearly identified?
<--- Score

48. What are your chatbots strategy processes?
<--- Score

49. What are the disruptive chatbots strategy technologies that enable your organization to radically change your business processes?
<--- Score

50. What qualifications and skills do you need?

<--- Score

51. How will corresponding data be collected?

<--- Score

52. What is the chatbots strategy Driver?

<--- Score

53. What do you need to qualify?

<--- Score

54. Do your contracts/agreements contain data security obligations?

<--- Score

55. Have the problem and goal statements been updated to reflect the additional knowledge gained from the analyze phase?

<--- Score

56. Is the performance gap determined?

<--- Score

57. How do you use chatbots strategy data and information to support organizational decision making and innovation?

<--- Score

58. How do you promote understanding that opportunity for improvement is not criticism of the status quo, or the people who created the status quo?

<--- Score

59. How do mission and objectives affect the chatbots strategy processes of your organization?

<--- Score

60. When should a process be art not science?
<--- Score

61. Does it help projection processes by improving R&D and forecasting?
<--- Score

62. What are your current levels and trends in key measures or indicators of chatbots strategy product and process performance that are important to and directly serve your customers? How do these results compare with the performance of your competitors and other organizations with similar offerings?
<--- Score

63. Is the suppliers process defined and controlled?
<--- Score

64. How was the detailed process map generated, verified, and validated?
<--- Score

65. What chatbots strategy data should be managed?
<--- Score

66. Is pre-qualification of suppliers carried out?
<--- Score

67. What are your key performance measures or indicators and in-process measures for the control and improvement of your chatbots strategy processes?
<--- Score

68. What qualifications are needed?

<--- Score

69. Who owns what data?
<--- Score

70. Is the gap/opportunity displayed and communicated in financial terms?
<--- Score

71. Was a detailed process map created to amplify critical steps of the 'as is' stakeholder process?
<--- Score

72. Who will gather what data?
<--- Score

73. What training and qualifications will you need?
<--- Score

74. What are your current levels and trends in key chatbots strategy measures or indicators of product and process performance that are important to and directly serve your customers?
<--- Score

75. What chatbots strategy data should be collected?
<--- Score

76. What data do you need to collect?
<--- Score

77. What chatbots strategy data will be collected?
<--- Score

78. Is the chatbots strategy process severely broken such that a re-design is necessary?

<--- Score

79. Are your outputs consistent?
<--- Score

80. Do several people in different organizational units assist with the chatbots strategy process?
<--- Score

81. How will the data be checked for quality?
<--- Score

82. What will drive chatbots strategy change?
<--- Score

83. What does the data say about the performance of the stakeholder process?
<--- Score

84. How many input/output points does it require?
<--- Score

85. What is the complexity of the output produced?
<--- Score

86. Have you defined which data is gathered how?
<--- Score

87. How do your work systems and key work processes relate to and capitalize on your core competencies?
<--- Score

88. How do you define collaboration and team output?
<--- Score

89. How has the chatbots strategy data been gathered?
<--- Score

90. Do you understand your management processes today?
<--- Score

91. How will the change process be managed?
<--- Score

92. What chatbots strategy metrics are outputs of the process?
<--- Score

93. Are all team members qualified for all tasks?
<--- Score

94. How can risk management be tied procedurally to process elements?
<--- Score

95. Is data and process analysis, root cause analysis and quantifying the gap/opportunity in place?
<--- Score

96. What are the best opportunities for value improvement?
<--- Score

97. Were there any improvement opportunities identified from the process analysis?
<--- Score

98. What is the cost of poor quality as supported by

the team's analysis?
<--- Score

99. Are all staff in core chatbots strategy subjects
Highly Qualified?
<--- Score

100. Where can you get qualified talent today?
<--- Score

101. What successful thing are you doing today that
may be blinding you to new growth opportunities?
<--- Score

102. What kind of crime could a potential new hire
have committed that would not only not disqualify
him/her from being hired by your organization,
but would actually indicate that he/she might be a
particularly good fit?
<--- Score

103. Is the required chatbots strategy data gathered?
<--- Score

104. What conclusions were drawn from the team's
data collection and analysis? How did the team reach
these conclusions?
<--- Score

105. How is data used for program management and
improvement?
<--- Score

106. What tools were used to narrow the list of
possible causes?
<--- Score

107. Do staff qualifications match your project?
<--- Score

108. What qualifies as competition?
<--- Score

109. What are evaluation criteria for the output?
<--- Score

110. What were the financial benefits resulting from any 'ground fruit or low-hanging fruit' (quick fixes)?
<--- Score

111. How is the data gathered?
<--- Score

112. What is the output?
<--- Score

113. What tools were used to generate the list of possible causes?
<--- Score

114. What data is gathered?
<--- Score

115. What qualifications do chatbots strategy leaders need?
<--- Score

116. How does the organization define, manage, and improve its chatbots strategy processes?
<--- Score

117. An organizationally feasible system request is

one that considers the mission, goals and objectives of the organization, key questions are: is the chatbots strategy solution request practical and will it solve a problem or take advantage of an opportunity to achieve company goals?

<--- Score

118. What methods do you use to gather chatbots strategy data?

<--- Score

119. Do you, as a leader, bounce back quickly from setbacks?

<--- Score

120. What process improvements will be needed?

<--- Score

121. What are the personnel training and qualifications required?

<--- Score

122. Is there a strict change management process?

<--- Score

123. What, related to, chatbots strategy processes does your organization outsource?

<--- Score

124. Should you invest in industry-recognized qualifications?

<--- Score

125. What is your organizations process which leads to recognition of value generation?

<--- Score

126. What types of data do your chatbots strategy indicators require?
<--- Score

127. What controls do you have in place to protect data?
<--- Score

128. How difficult is it to qualify what chatbots strategy ROI is?
<--- Score

129. What are the necessary qualifications?
<--- Score

130. Can you add value to the current chatbots strategy decision-making process (largely qualitative) by incorporating uncertainty modeling (more quantitative)?
<--- Score

131. Were Pareto charts (or similar) used to portray the 'heavy hitters' (or key sources of variation)?
<--- Score

132. How much data can be collected in the given timeframe?
<--- Score

133. Who qualifies to gain access to data?
<--- Score

Add up total points for this section:
_ _ _ _ _ = Total points for this section

Divided by: _____ (number of
statements answered) = _____
Average score for this section

Transfer your score to the chatbots
strategy Index at the beginning of the
Self-Assessment.

CRITERION #5: IMPROVE:

1. At what point will vulnerability assessments
be performed once chatbots strategy is put into
production (e.g., ongoing Risk Management after
implementation)?
<--- Score

2. Risk events: what are the things that could go
wrong?
<--- Score

3. What are the affordable chatbots strategy risks?
<--- Score

4. Would you develop a chatbots strategy Communication Strategy?
<--- Score

5. How do you keep improving chatbots strategy?
<--- Score

6. If you could go back in time five years, what decision would you make differently? What is your best guess as to what decision you're making today you might regret five years from now?
<--- Score

7. Why improve in the first place?
<--- Score

8. How scalable is your chatbots strategy solution?
<--- Score

9. For decision problems, how do you develop a decision statement?
<--- Score

10. When you map the key players in your own work and the types/domains of relationships with them, which relationships do you find easy and which challenging, and why?
<--- Score

11. How will you recognize and celebrate results?
<--- Score

12. What is chatbots strategy risk?
<--- Score

13. Who manages chatbots strategy risk?
<--- Score

14. How do you manage chatbots strategy risk?
<--- Score

15. How will you know when its improved?
<--- Score

16. What error proofing will be done to address some of the discrepancies observed in the 'as is' process?
<--- Score

17. What is the magnitude of the improvements?
<--- Score

18. What needs improvement? Why?
<--- Score

19. What area needs the greatest improvement?
<--- Score

20. What practices helps your organization to develop its capacity to recognize patterns?
<--- Score

21. Are decisions made in a timely manner?
<--- Score

22. Who are the chatbots strategy decision makers?
<--- Score

23. What tools were most useful during the improve

phase?
<--- Score

24. Does a good decision guarantee a good outcome?
<--- Score

25. What are your current levels and trends in key measures or indicators of workforce and leader development?
<--- Score

26. What is the team's contingency plan for potential problems occurring in implementation?
<--- Score

27. Are you assessing chatbots strategy and risk?
<--- Score

28. Do vendor agreements bring new compliance risk ?
<--- Score

29. Do you have the optimal project management team structure?
<--- Score

30. What tools were used to evaluate the potential solutions?
<--- Score

31. Is the chatbots strategy risk managed?
<--- Score

32. Is any chatbots strategy documentation required?
<--- Score

33. Is the scope clearly documented?
<--- Score

34. How do you manage and improve your chatbots strategy work systems to deliver customer value and achieve organizational success and sustainability?
<--- Score

35. Are the risks fully understood, reasonable and manageable?
<--- Score

36. How do you define the solutions' scope?
<--- Score

37. What improvements have been achieved?
<--- Score

38. What are the chatbots strategy security risks?
<--- Score

39. How is continuous improvement applied to risk management?
<--- Score

40. Have you identified breakpoints and/or risk tolerances that will trigger broad consideration of a potential need for intervention or modification of strategy?
<--- Score

41. How do you measure improved chatbots strategy service perception, and satisfaction?
<--- Score

42. How are policy decisions made and where?

<--- Score

43. What are the expected chatbots strategy results?
<--- Score

44. Who controls the risk?
<--- Score

45. Which chatbots strategy solution is appropriate?
<--- Score

46. How do you improve chatbots strategy service perception, and satisfaction?
<--- Score

47. Who will be responsible for documenting the chatbots strategy requirements in detail?
<--- Score

48. What is the implementation plan?
<--- Score

49. How do the chatbots strategy results compare with the performance of your competitors and other organizations with similar offerings?
<--- Score

50. chatbots strategy risk decisions: whose call Is It?
<--- Score

51. What risks do you need to manage?
<--- Score

52. Who are the key stakeholders for the chatbots strategy evaluation?
<--- Score

53. What can you do to improve?
<--- Score

54. How does the team improve its work?
<--- Score

55. What is chatbots strategy's impact on utilizing the best solution(s)?
<--- Score

56. What alternative responses are available to manage risk?
<--- Score

57. Where do the chatbots strategy decisions reside?
<--- Score

58. What assumptions are made about the solution and approach?
<--- Score

59. Do you need to do a usability evaluation?
<--- Score

60. Is there a high likelihood that any recommendations will achieve their intended results?
<--- Score

61. Who manages supplier risk management in your organization?
<--- Score

62. Who are the people involved in developing and implementing chatbots strategy?
<--- Score

63. Explorations of the frontiers of chatbots strategy will help you build influence, improve chatbots strategy, optimize decision making, and sustain change, what is your approach?
<--- Score

64. What are the implications of the one critical chatbots strategy decision 10 minutes, 10 months, and 10 years from now?
<--- Score

65. What current systems have to be understood and/or changed?
<--- Score

66. Who controls key decisions that will be made?
<--- Score

67. How do you go about comparing chatbots strategy approaches/solutions?
<--- Score

68. Who will be responsible for making the decisions to include or exclude requested changes once chatbots strategy is underway?
<--- Score

69. How will you measure the results?
<--- Score

70. How is the chatbots strategy Value Stream Mapping managed?
<--- Score

71. What is the chatbots strategy's sustainability risk?

<--- Score

72. Do you cover the five essential competencies: Communication, Collaboration,Innovation, Adaptability, and Leadership that improve an organizations ability to leverage the new chatbots strategy in a volatile global economy?
<--- Score

73. Can you identify any significant risks or exposures to chatbots strategy third- parties (vendors, service providers, alliance partners etc) that concern you?
<--- Score

74. Are the most efficient solutions problem-specific?
<--- Score

75. Does the goal represent a desired result that can be measured?
<--- Score

76. How do you deal with chatbots strategy risk?
<--- Score

77. Are procedures documented for managing chatbots strategy risks?
<--- Score

78. Are risk management tasks balanced centrally and locally?
<--- Score

79. Is the measure of success for chatbots strategy understandable to a variety of people?
<--- Score

80. What to do with the results or outcomes of measurements?
<--- Score

81. What does the 'should be' process map/design look like?
<--- Score

82. Was a chatbots strategy charter developed?
<--- Score

83. How do you measure risk?
<--- Score

84. Are the key business and technology risks being managed?
<--- Score

85. What criteria will you use to assess your chatbots strategy risks?
<--- Score

86. Is chatbots strategy documentation maintained?
<--- Score

87. To what extent does management recognize chatbots strategy as a tool to increase the results?
<--- Score

88. What tools do you use once you have decided on a chatbots strategy strategy and more importantly how do you choose?
<--- Score

89. What actually has to improve and by how much?
<--- Score

90. Do those selected for the chatbots strategy team have a good general understanding of what chatbots strategy is all about?
<--- Score

91. How are chatbots strategy risks managed?
<--- Score

92. How can the phases of chatbots strategy development be identified?
<--- Score

93. How do you link measurement and risk?
<--- Score

94. How is knowledge sharing about risk management improved?
<--- Score

95. Who makes the chatbots strategy decisions in your organization?
<--- Score

96. What should a proof of concept or pilot accomplish?
<--- Score

97. Is the solution technically practical?
<--- Score

98. Will the controls trigger any other risks?
<--- Score

99. Risk factors: what are the characteristics of chatbots strategy that make it risky?

<--- Score

100. What are the concrete chatbots strategy results?
<--- Score

101. Who do you report chatbots strategy results to?
<--- Score

102. Is the chatbots strategy solution sustainable?
<--- Score

103. How will you know that a change is an improvement?
<--- Score

104. What went well, what should change, what can improve?
<--- Score

105. What resources are required for the improvement efforts?
<--- Score

106. What is the risk?
<--- Score

107. Risk Identification: What are the possible risk events your organization faces in relation to chatbots strategy?
<--- Score

108. In the past few months, what is the smallest change you have made that has had the biggest positive result? What was it about that small change that produced the large return?
<--- Score

109. For estimation problems, how do you develop an estimation statement?
<--- Score

110. Is supporting chatbots strategy documentation required?
<--- Score

111. Can you integrate quality management and risk management?
<--- Score

112. What were the criteria for evaluating a chatbots strategy pilot?
<--- Score

113. What were the underlying assumptions on the cost-benefit analysis?
<--- Score

114. How does your organization evaluate strategic chatbots strategy success?
<--- Score

115. Have you achieved chatbots strategy improvements?
<--- Score

116. Which of the recognised risks out of all risks can be most likely transferred?
<--- Score

117. Are risk triggers captured?
<--- Score

118. What lessons, if any, from a pilot were incorporated into the design of the full-scale solution?
<--- Score

119. Is there any other chatbots strategy solution?
<--- Score

120. What strategies for chatbots strategy improvement are successful?
<--- Score

121. How risky is your organization?
<--- Score

122. How can you better manage risk?
<--- Score

123. Can the solution be designed and implemented within an acceptable time period?
<--- Score

124. How do you decide how much to remunerate an employee?
<--- Score

125. Who will be using the results of the measurement activities?
<--- Score

126. Who are the chatbots strategy decision-makers?
<--- Score

127. What tools were used to tap into the creativity and encourage 'outside the box' thinking?
<--- Score

128. Is risk periodically assessed?
<--- Score

129. Where do you need chatbots strategy improvement?
<--- Score

130. How can you improve chatbots strategy?
<--- Score

131. Is the chatbots strategy documentation thorough?
<--- Score

132. How do you improve productivity?
<--- Score

133. How can you improve performance?
<--- Score

134. How do you measure progress and evaluate training effectiveness?
<--- Score

135. How can skill-level changes improve chatbots strategy?
<--- Score

136. How will you know that you have improved?
<--- Score

137. How significant is the improvement in the eyes of the end user?
<--- Score

Add up total points for this section:

_____ = Total points for this section

Divided by: _____ (number of
statements answered) = _____
Average score for this section

Transfer your score to the chatbots
strategy Index at the beginning of the
Self-Assessment.

CRITERION #6: CONTROL:

INTENT: Implement the practical solution. Maintain the performance and correct possible complications.

In my belief, the answer to this question is clearly defined:

5 Strongly Agree

4 Agree

3 Neutral

2 Disagree

1 Strongly Disagree

1. How will the process owner and team be able to hold the gains?
<--- Score

2. Are you measuring, monitoring and predicting chatbots strategy activities to optimize operations and profitability, and enhancing outcomes?
<--- Score

3. Is there documentation that will support the successful operation of the improvement?
<--- Score

4. You may have created your quality measures at a time when you lacked resources, technology wasn't up to the required standard, or low service levels were the industry norm. Have those circumstances changed?
<--- Score

5. Are new process steps, standards, and documentation ingrained into normal operations?
<--- Score

6. What do your reports reflect?
<--- Score

7. Who has control over resources?
<--- Score

8. Who will be in control?
<--- Score

9. Does job training on the documented procedures need to be part of the process team's education and training?
<--- Score

10. Will existing staff require re-training, for example, to learn new business processes?
<--- Score

11. Act/Adjust: What Do you Need to Do Differently?
<--- Score

12. What do you measure to verify effectiveness gains?
<--- Score

13. Are documented procedures clear and easy to follow for the operators?
<--- Score

14. What should you measure to verify efficiency gains?
<--- Score

15. Will any special training be provided for results interpretation?
<--- Score

16. Are the planned controls in place?
<--- Score

17. Do the viable solutions scale to future needs?
<--- Score

18. How do controls support value?
<--- Score

19. Is there a standardized process?
<--- Score

20. What key inputs and outputs are being measured on an ongoing basis?
<--- Score

21. What are the key elements of your chatbots strategy performance improvement system, including your evaluation, organizational learning, and innovation processes?

<--- Score

22. What are your results for key measures or indicators of the accomplishment of your chatbots strategy strategy and action plans, including building and strengthening core competencies?
<--- Score

23. Who is going to spread your message?
<--- Score

24. How might the group capture best practices and lessons learned so as to leverage improvements?
<--- Score

25. How do senior leaders actions reflect a commitment to the organizations chatbots strategy values?
<--- Score

26. Is a response plan established and deployed?
<--- Score

27. Is a response plan in place for when the input, process, or output measures indicate an 'out-of-control' condition?
<--- Score

28. How do your controls stack up?
<--- Score

29. What do you stand for--and what are you against?
<--- Score

30. How will input, process, and output variables be checked to detect for sub-optimal conditions?

<--- Score

31. How do you plan on providing proper recognition and disclosure of supporting companies?
<--- Score

32. What should the next improvement project be that is related to chatbots strategy?
<--- Score

33. Do you monitor the effectiveness of your chatbots strategy activities?
<--- Score

34. Who sets the chatbots strategy standards?
<--- Score

35. Do you monitor the chatbots strategy decisions made and fine tune them as they evolve?
<--- Score

36. Will the team be available to assist members in planning investigations?
<--- Score

37. Is reporting being used or needed?
<--- Score

38. How is change control managed?
<--- Score

39. Is there a transfer of ownership and knowledge to process owner and process team tasked with the responsibilities.
<--- Score

40. Does chatbots strategy appropriately measure and monitor risk?

<--- Score

41. Has the improved process and its steps been standardized?

<--- Score

42. What is the best design framework for chatbots strategy organization now that, in a post industrial-age if the top-down, command and control model is no longer relevant?

<--- Score

43. How will you measure your QA plan's effectiveness?

<--- Score

44. What is the recommended frequency of auditing?

<--- Score

45. Is there a control plan in place for sustaining improvements (short and long-term)?

<--- Score

46. What chatbots strategy standards are applicable?

<--- Score

47. Is there a chatbots strategy Communication plan covering who needs to get what information when?

<--- Score

48. Does the chatbots strategy performance meet the customer's requirements?

<--- Score

49. Are pertinent alerts monitored, analyzed and distributed to appropriate personnel?
<--- Score

50. Are the chatbots strategy standards challenging?
<--- Score

51. Are the planned controls working?
<--- Score

52. What are the critical parameters to watch?
<--- Score

53. How can you best use all of your knowledge repositories to enhance learning and sharing?
<--- Score

54. Does the response plan contain a definite closed loop continual improvement scheme (e.g., plan-do-check-act)?
<--- Score

55. Are suggested corrective/restorative actions indicated on the response plan for known causes to problems that might surface?
<--- Score

56. Is there a recommended audit plan for routine surveillance inspections of chatbots strategy's gains?
<--- Score

57. Does a troubleshooting guide exist or is it needed?
<--- Score

58. How will new or emerging customer needs/requirements be checked/communicated to orient

the process toward meeting the new specifications and continually reducing variation?
<--- Score

59. Is the chatbots strategy test/monitoring cost justified?
<--- Score

60. Do the chatbots strategy decisions you make today help people and the planet tomorrow?
<--- Score

61. How will the day-to-day responsibilities for monitoring and continual improvement be transferred from the improvement team to the process owner?
<--- Score

62. Who controls critical resources?
<--- Score

63. How do you select, collect, align, and integrate chatbots strategy data and information for tracking daily operations and overall organizational performance, including progress relative to strategic objectives and action plans?
<--- Score

64. How will report readings be checked to effectively monitor performance?
<--- Score

65. How likely is the current chatbots strategy plan to come in on schedule or on budget?
<--- Score

66. Has the chatbots strategy value of standards been quantified?
<--- Score

67. Is knowledge gained on process shared and institutionalized?
<--- Score

68. What other systems, operations, processes, and infrastructures (hiring practices, staffing, training, incentives/rewards, metrics/dashboards/scorecards, etc.) need updates, additions, changes, or deletions in order to facilitate knowledge transfer and improvements?
<--- Score

69. Can you adapt and adjust to changing chatbots strategy situations?
<--- Score

70. Implementation Planning: is a pilot needed to test the changes before a full roll out occurs?
<--- Score

71. Is new knowledge gained imbedded in the response plan?
<--- Score

72. How do you plan for the cost of succession?
<--- Score

73. In the case of a chatbots strategy project, the criteria for the audit derive from implementation objectives, an audit of a chatbots strategy project involves assessing whether the recommendations outlined for implementation have been met, can

you track that any chatbots strategy project is implemented as planned, and is it working?
<--- Score

74. How do you spread information?
<--- Score

75. How do you encourage people to take control and responsibility?
<--- Score

76. How do you monitor usage and cost?
<--- Score

77. Can support from partners be adjusted?
<--- Score

78. What are you attempting to measure/monitor?
<--- Score

79. Are controls in place and consistently applied?
<--- Score

80. Who is the chatbots strategy process owner?
<--- Score

81. Is there a documented and implemented monitoring plan?
<--- Score

82. Are there documented procedures?
<--- Score

83. Will your goals reflect your program budget?
<--- Score

84. What is the standard for acceptable chatbots strategy performance?
<--- Score

85. What is the control/monitoring plan?
<--- Score

86. How is chatbots strategy project cost planned, managed, monitored?
<--- Score

87. What is your plan to assess your security risks?
<--- Score

88. Are operating procedures consistent?
<--- Score

89. How will the process owner verify improvement in present and future sigma levels, process capabilities?
<--- Score

90. Against what alternative is success being measured?
<--- Score

91. Where do ideas that reach policy makers and planners as proposals for chatbots strategy strengthening and reform actually originate?
<--- Score

92. Have new or revised work instructions resulted?
<--- Score

93. What can you control?
<--- Score

94. What are the performance and scale of the chatbots strategy tools?
<--- Score

95. How widespread is its use?
<--- Score

96. What quality tools were useful in the control phase?
<--- Score

97. How do you establish and deploy modified action plans if circumstances require a shift in plans and rapid execution of new plans?
<--- Score

98. What is your theory of human motivation, and how does your compensation plan fit with that view?
<--- Score

99. What are customers monitoring?
<--- Score

100. What are the known security controls?
<--- Score

101. What other areas of the group might benefit from the chatbots strategy team's improvements, knowledge, and learning?
<--- Score

102. Is there an action plan in case of emergencies?
<--- Score

Add up total points for this section:
_ _ _ _ _ = Total points for this section

Divided by: _____ (number of
statements answered) = _____
Average score for this section

Transfer your score to the chatbots
strategy Index at the beginning of the
Self-Assessment.

CRITERION #7: SUSTAIN:

INTENT: Retain the benefits.

In my belief, the answer to this
question is clearly defined:

5 Strongly Agree

4 Agree

3 Neutral

2 Disagree

1 Strongly Disagree

1. What have been your experiences in defining long
range chatbots strategy goals?
<--- Score

2. At what moment would you think; Will I get fired?
<--- Score

3. How do you keep the momentum going?
<--- Score

4. Are you making progress, and are you making

progress as chatbots strategy leaders?
<--- Score

5. Is the impact that chatbots strategy has shown?
<--- Score

6. Instead of going to current contacts for new ideas, what if you reconnected with dormant contacts-- the people you used to know? If you were going reactivate a dormant tie, who would it be?
<--- Score

7. How can you negotiate chatbots strategy successfully with a stubborn boss, an irate client, or a deceitful coworker?
<--- Score

8. If you got fired and a new hire took your place, what would she do different?
<--- Score

9. What are the long-term chatbots strategy goals?
<--- Score

10. Are you paying enough attention to the partners your company depends on to succeed?
<--- Score

11. Are you maintaining a past–present–future perspective throughout the chatbots strategy discussion?
<--- Score

12. Who will provide the final approval of chatbots strategy deliverables?
<--- Score

13. Did your employees make progress today?
<--- Score

14. Who do you want your customers to become?
<--- Score

15. Who is the main stakeholder, with ultimate responsibility for driving chatbots strategy forward?
<--- Score

16. How does chatbots strategy integrate with other stakeholder initiatives?
<--- Score

17. What is the recommended frequency of auditing?
<--- Score

18. Where can you break convention?
<--- Score

19. Can the schedule be done in the given time?
<--- Score

20. Are you using a design thinking approach and integrating Innovation, chatbots strategy Experience, and Brand Value?
<--- Score

21. What information is critical to your organization that your executives are ignoring?
<--- Score

22. Political -is anyone trying to undermine this project?
<--- Score

23. What chatbots strategy modifications can you make work for you?
<--- Score

24. What stupid rule would you most like to kill?
<--- Score

25. Who are four people whose careers you have enhanced?
<--- Score

26. Have new benefits been realized?
<--- Score

27. Is there any reason to believe the opposite of my current belief?
<--- Score

28. Who, on the executive team or the board, has spoken to a customer recently?
<--- Score

29. What are the challenges?
<--- Score

30. If you weren't already in this business, would you enter it today? And if not, what are you going to do about it?
<--- Score

31. What is the big chatbots strategy idea?
<--- Score

32. Do you see more potential in people than they do in themselves?

<--- Score

33. What chatbots strategy skills are most important?
<--- Score

34. In the past year, what have you done (or could you have done) to increase the accurate perception of your company/brand as ethical and honest?
<--- Score

35. How do you stay inspired?
<--- Score

36. Do you have past chatbots strategy successes?
<--- Score

37. What did you miss in the interview for the worst hire you ever made?
<--- Score

38. What have you done to protect your business from competitive encroachment?
<--- Score

39. How do you make it meaningful in connecting chatbots strategy with what users do day-to-day?
<--- Score

40. Are the assumptions believable and achievable?
<--- Score

41. Are your responses positive or negative?
<--- Score

42. What are the key enablers to make this chatbots strategy move?

<--- Score

43. What does your signature ensure?
<--- Score

44. What are the top 3 things at the forefront of your chatbots strategy agendas for the next 3 years?
<--- Score

45. Who have you, as a company, historically been when you've been at your best?
<--- Score

46. Why not do chatbots strategy?
<--- Score

47. Is chatbots strategy dependent on the successful delivery of a current project?
<--- Score

48. What happens when a new employee joins the organization?
<--- Score

49. Is there any existing chatbots strategy governance structure?
<--- Score

50. What trouble can you get into?
<--- Score

51. Is it economical; do you have the time and money?
<--- Score

52. What would you recommend your friend do if he/she were facing this dilemma?

<--- Score

53. How can you become the company that would put you out of business?
<--- Score

54. How do you foster innovation?
<--- Score

55. How do you transition from the baseline to the target?
<--- Score

56. What are current chatbots strategy paradigms?
<--- Score

57. If you had to rebuild your organization without any traditional competitive advantages (i.e., no killer technology, promising research, innovative product/ service delivery model, etcetera), how would your people have to approach their work and collaborate together in order to create the necessary conditions for success?
<--- Score

58. What role does communication play in the success or failure of a chatbots strategy project?
<--- Score

59. Is your basic point _____ or _____?
<--- Score

60. What are the success criteria that will indicate that chatbots strategy objectives have been met and the benefits delivered?
<--- Score

61. If you do not follow, then how to lead?
<--- Score

62. How long will it take to change?
<--- Score

63. How do you govern and fulfill your societal responsibilities?
<--- Score

64. What is your question? Why?
<--- Score

65. What are the essentials of internal chatbots strategy management?
<--- Score

66. Ask yourself: how would you do this work if you only had one staff member to do it?
<--- Score

67. Who will manage the integration of tools?
<--- Score

68. What is the funding source for this project?
<--- Score

69. Do you have an implicit bias for capital investments over people investments?
<--- Score

70. What happens if you do not have enough funding?
<--- Score

71. How do you assess the chatbots strategy pitfalls that are inherent in implementing it?
<--- Score

72. Who uses your product in ways you never expected?
<--- Score

73. What potential megatrends could make your business model obsolete?
<--- Score

74. What one word do you want to own in the minds of your customers, employees, and partners?
<--- Score

75. How will you motivate the stakeholders with the least vested interest?
<--- Score

76. What is the craziest thing you can do?
<--- Score

77. Why do and why don't your customers like your organization?
<--- Score

78. What is the overall business strategy?
<--- Score

79. If you had to leave your organization for a year and the only communication you could have with employees/colleagues was a single paragraph, what would you write?
<--- Score

80. What knowledge, skills and characteristics mark a good chatbots strategy project manager?
<--- Score

81. Why is chatbots strategy important for you now?
<--- Score

82. What is the kind of project structure that would be appropriate for your chatbots strategy project, should it be formal and complex, or can it be less formal and relatively simple?
<--- Score

83. Which functions and people interact with the supplier and or customer?
<--- Score

84. What would have to be true for the option on the table to be the best possible choice?
<--- Score

85. How can you become more high-tech but still be high touch?
<--- Score

86. How do you engage the workforce, in addition to satisfying them?
<--- Score

87. If your company went out of business tomorrow, would anyone who doesn't get a paycheck here care?
<--- Score

88. If you were responsible for initiating and implementing major changes in your organization, what steps might you take to ensure acceptance of

those changes?
<--- Score

89. What management system can you use to leverage the chatbots strategy experience, ideas, and concerns of the people closest to the work to be done?
<--- Score

90. How do you listen to customers to obtain actionable information?
<--- Score

91. Are you satisfied with your current role? If not, what is missing from it?
<--- Score

92. Which models, tools and techniques are necessary?
<--- Score

93. What you are going to do to affect the numbers?
<--- Score

94. Is there a work around that you can use?
<--- Score

95. How can you incorporate support to ensure safe and effective use of chatbots strategy into the services that you provide?
<--- Score

96. Is a chatbots strategy team work effort in place?
<--- Score

97. Whose voice (department, ethnic group, women,

older workers, etc) might you have missed hearing from in your company, and how might you amplify this voice to create positive momentum for your business?

<--- Score

98. Which chatbots strategy goals are the most important?

<--- Score

99. What could happen if you do not do it?

<--- Score

100. What counts that you are not counting?

<--- Score

101. What are the usability implications of chatbots strategy actions?

<--- Score

102. Who is responsible for ensuring appropriate resources (time, people and money) are allocated to chatbots strategy?

<--- Score

103. What are the barriers to increased chatbots strategy production?

<--- Score

104. How do you accomplish your long range chatbots strategy goals?

<--- Score

105. Do you know what you are doing? And who do you call if you don't?

<--- Score

106. When information truly is ubiquitous, when reach and connectivity are completely global, when computing resources are infinite, and when a whole new set of impossibilities are not only possible, but happening, what will that do to your business?
<--- Score

107. What are your personal philosophies regarding chatbots strategy and how do they influence your work?
<--- Score

108. What are the potential basics of chatbots strategy fraud?
<--- Score

109. Has implementation been effective in reaching specified objectives so far?
<--- Score

110. If no one would ever find out about your accomplishments, how would you lead differently?
<--- Score

111. What was the last experiment you ran?
<--- Score

112. What is an unauthorized commitment?
<--- Score

113. Is maximizing chatbots strategy protection the same as minimizing chatbots strategy loss?
<--- Score

114. How will you ensure you get what you expected?

<--- Score

115. What do you do to operate securely within cloud environments while at work?
<--- Score

116. How do you create buy-in?
<--- Score

117. What are you trying to prove to yourself, and how might it be hijacking your life and business success?
<--- Score

118. What should you stop doing?
<--- Score

119. Would you rather sell to knowledgeable and informed customers or to uninformed customers?
<--- Score

120. Why should you adopt a chatbots strategy framework?
<--- Score

121. What unique value proposition (UVP) do you offer?
<--- Score

122. Do you know who is a friend or a foe?
<--- Score

123. Can you do all this work?
<--- Score

124. Can you maintain your growth without detracting from the factors that have contributed to

your success?
<--- Score

125. What relationships among chatbots strategy trends do you perceive?
<--- Score

126. To whom do you add value?
<--- Score

127. Is chatbots strategy realistic, or are you setting yourself up for failure?
<--- Score

128. Who do you think the world wants your organization to be?
<--- Score

129. What happens at your organization when people fail?
<--- Score

130. How do you manage chatbots strategy Knowledge Management (KM)?
<--- Score

131. If there were zero limitations, what would you do differently?
<--- Score

132. Do you have enough freaky customers in your portfolio pushing you to the limit day in and day out?
<--- Score

133. Are the criteria for selecting recommendations stated?

<--- Score

134. How do you keep records, of what?
<--- Score

135. What is the source of the strategies for chatbots strategy strengthening and reform?
<--- Score

136. Are you changing as fast as the world around you?
<--- Score

137. What is the estimated value of the project?
<--- Score

138. What must you excel at?
<--- Score

139. What is it like to work for you?
<--- Score

140. How is implementation research currently incorporated into each of your goals?
<--- Score

141. Who is on the team?
<--- Score

142. Is the chatbots strategy organization completing tasks effectively and efficiently?
<--- Score

143. Are new benefits received and understood?
<--- Score

144. What do we do when new problems arise?
<--- Score

145. How important is chatbots strategy to the user organizations mission?
<--- Score

146. Do chatbots strategy rules make a reasonable demand on a users capabilities?
<--- Score

147. How do you track customer value, profitability or financial return, organizational success, and sustainability?
<--- Score

148. Do you have the right capabilities and capacities?
<--- Score

149. Why will customers want to buy your organizations products/services?
<--- Score

150. Which individuals, teams or departments will be involved in chatbots strategy?
<--- Score

151. If your customer were your grandmother, would you tell her to buy what you're selling?
<--- Score

152. What is the overall talent health of your organization as a whole at senior levels, and for each organization reporting to a member of the Senior Leadership Team?
<--- Score

153. Who will be responsible for deciding whether chatbots strategy goes ahead or not after the initial investigations?
<--- Score

154. Is your strategy driving your strategy? Or is the way in which you allocate resources driving your strategy?
<--- Score

155. Are you / should you be revolutionary or evolutionary?
<--- Score

156. How do you maintain chatbots strategy's Integrity?
<--- Score

157. What are the gaps in your knowledge and experience?
<--- Score

158. Who are your customers?
<--- Score

159. What will be the consequences to the stakeholder (financial, reputation etc) if chatbots strategy does not go ahead or fails to deliver the objectives?
<--- Score

160. Who else should you help?
<--- Score

161. How do customers see your organization?

<--- Score

162. How do you know if you are successful?
<--- Score

163. What are the rules and assumptions your industry operates under? What if the opposite were true?
<--- Score

164. How much does chatbots strategy help?
<--- Score

165. What is a feasible sequencing of reform initiatives over time?
<--- Score

166. Who is responsible for errors?
<--- Score

167. Will it be accepted by users?
<--- Score

168. What threat is chatbots strategy addressing?
<--- Score

169. What is your competitive advantage?
<--- Score

170. Why is it important to have senior management support for a chatbots strategy project?
<--- Score

171. Do you feel that more should be done in the chatbots strategy area?
<--- Score

172. What goals did you miss?
<--- Score

173. Are there any activities that you can take off your to do list?
<--- Score

174. Who are the key stakeholders?
<--- Score

175. Why should people listen to you?
<--- Score

176. What are internal and external chatbots strategy relations?
<--- Score

177. What are the business goals chatbots strategy is aiming to achieve?
<--- Score

178. How do you set chatbots strategy stretch targets and how do you get people to not only participate in setting these stretch targets but also that they strive to achieve these?
<--- Score

179. Will there be any necessary staff changes (redundancies or new hires)?
<--- Score

180. What is your chatbots strategy strategy?
<--- Score

181. Are you relevant? Will you be relevant five years from now? Ten?

<--- Score

182. How much contingency will be available in the budget?
<--- Score

183. What is your formula for success in chatbots strategy ?
<--- Score

184. Are all key stakeholders present at all Structured Walkthroughs?
<--- Score

185. Are assumptions made in chatbots strategy stated explicitly?
<--- Score

186. How will you insure seamless interoperability of chatbots strategy moving forward?
<--- Score

187. Have benefits been optimized with all key stakeholders?
<--- Score

188. How do you provide a safe environment -physically and emotionally?
<--- Score

189. What is effective chatbots strategy?
<--- Score

190. How do you foster the skills, knowledge, talents, attributes, and characteristics you want to have?
<--- Score

191. Operational - will it work?
<--- Score

192. How do you deal with chatbots strategy changes?
<--- Score

193. How do you determine the key elements that affect chatbots strategy workforce satisfaction, how are these elements determined for different workforce groups and segments?
<--- Score

194. Do you have the right people on the bus?
<--- Score

195. What is the purpose of chatbots strategy in relation to the mission?
<--- Score

196. What new services of functionality will be implemented next with chatbots strategy ?
<--- Score

197. Do you think chatbots strategy accomplishes the goals you expect it to accomplish?
<--- Score

198. What projects are going on in the organization today, and what resources are those projects using from the resource pools?
<--- Score

199. What may be the consequences for the performance of an organization if all stakeholders are

not consulted regarding chatbots strategy?
<--- Score

200. What are you challenging?
<--- Score

201. Who will determine interim and final deadlines?
<--- Score

202. Can you break it down?
<--- Score

203. In a project to restructure chatbots strategy outcomes, which stakeholders would you involve?
<--- Score

204. How will you know that the chatbots strategy project has been successful?
<--- Score

205. How do you cross-sell and up-sell your chatbots strategy success?
<--- Score

206. Do you think you know, or do you know you know ?
<--- Score

207. Who is responsible for chatbots strategy?
<--- Score

208. How do you go about securing chatbots strategy?
<--- Score

209. How do you lead with chatbots strategy in mind?

<--- Score

210. Who do we want your customers to become?
<--- Score

211. Are you now in the promised land of great Customer experience?
<--- Score

212. Were lessons learned captured and communicated?
<--- Score

213. How likely is it that a customer would recommend your company to a friend or colleague?
<--- Score

214. What is something you believe that nearly no one agrees with you on?
<--- Score

215. How do you proactively clarify deliverables and chatbots strategy quality expectations?
<--- Score

Add up total points for this section:
_ _ _ _ _   = Total points for this section

Divided by: _ _ _ _ _ _ (number of statements answered) = _ _ _ _ _ _
Average score for this section

Transfer your score to the chatbots strategy Index at the beginning of the Self-Assessment.

Chatbots Strategy and Managing Projects, Criteria for Project Managers:

1.0 Initiating Process Group: Chatbots Strategy

1. Realistic - are the desired results expressed in a way that the team will be motivated and believe that the required level of involvement will be obtained?

2. What technical work to do in each phase?

3. Did the Chatbots Strategy project team have the right skills?

4. Will the Chatbots Strategy project meet the client requirements, and will it achieve the business success criteria that justified doing the Chatbots Strategy project in the first place?

5. Have the stakeholders identified all individual requirements pertaining to business process?

6. What are the tools and techniques to be used in each phase?

7. Mitigate. what will you do to minimize the impact should the risk event occur?

8. How well did you do?

9. Were resources available as planned?

10. The Chatbots Strategy project managers have maximum authority in which type of organization?

11. Contingency planning. if a risk event occurs, what will you do?

12. If action is called for, what form should it take?

13. How will it affect me?

14. Who is behind the Chatbots Strategy project?

15. What is the stake of others in your Chatbots Strategy project?

16. Information sharing?

17. In which Chatbots Strategy project management process group is the detailed Chatbots Strategy project budget created?

18. Who supports, improves, and oversees standardized processes related to the Chatbots Strategy projects program?

19. What are the required resources?

20. How well defined and documented were the Chatbots Strategy project management processes you chose to use?

1.1 Project Charter: Chatbots Strategy

21. How much?

22. Chatbots Strategy project background: what is the primary motivation for this Chatbots Strategy project?

23. If finished, on what date did it finish?

24. What is the most common tool for helping define the detail?

25. Success determination factors: how will the success of the Chatbots Strategy project be determined from the customers perspective?

26. Strategic fit: what is the strategic initiative identifier for this Chatbots Strategy project?

27. Customer benefits: what customer requirements does this Chatbots Strategy project address?

28. Customer: who are you doing the Chatbots Strategy project for?

29. What are the constraints?

30. What are the assumptions?

31. Who ise input and support will this Chatbots Strategy project require?

32. Pop quiz – which are the same inputs as in the Chatbots Strategy project charter?

33. When will this occur?

34. Why executive support?

35. Why the improvements?

36. What does it need to do?

37. For whom?

38. Why is a Chatbots Strategy project Charter used?

39. Who is the sponsor?

40. Who manages integration?

1.2 Stakeholder Register: Chatbots Strategy

41. What opportunities exist to provide communications?

42. How should employers make voices heard?

43. Who is managing stakeholder engagement?

44. How big is the gap?

45. Who wants to talk about Security?

46. How much influence do they have on the Chatbots Strategy project?

47. Who are the stakeholders?

48. What & Why?

49. Is your organization ready for change?

50. What are the major Chatbots Strategy project milestones requiring communications or providing communications opportunities?

51. What is the power of the stakeholder?

52. How will reports be created?

1.3 Stakeholder Analysis Matrix: Chatbots Strategy

53. How will the Chatbots Strategy project benefit them?

54. Why is it important to identify them?

55. Processes and systems, etc?

56. How do rules, behaviors affect stakes?

57. Where are the good opportunities facing your organizations development?

58. Which conditions out of the control of the management are crucial for the achievement of the outputs?

59. Who will be affected by the work?

60. Location and geographical?

61. Timescales, deadlines and pressures?

62. New technologies, services, ideas?

63. What is accountability in relation to the Chatbots Strategy project?

64. How to measure the achievement of the Development Objective?

65. Is there a reason why you are or are not not using an external rating system?

66. Which conditions out of the control of the management are crucial to contribute for the achievement of the development objective?

67. Is changing technology threatening your organizations position?

68. What could your organization improve?

69. What do you Evaluate?

70. What can the Chatbots Strategy projects outcome be used for?

71. Who is directly responsible for decisions on issues important to the Chatbots Strategy project?

72. Tactics: eg, surprise, major contracts?

2.0 Planning Process Group: Chatbots Strategy

73. Are the necessary foundations in place to ensure the sustainability of the results of the Chatbots Strategy project?

74. How many days can task X be late in starting without affecting the Chatbots Strategy project completion date?

75. What is involved in Chatbots Strategy project scope management, and why is good Chatbots Strategy project scope management so important on information technology Chatbots Strategy projects?

76. You are creating your WBS and find that you keep decomposing tasks into smaller and smaller units. How can you tell when you are done?

77. The Chatbots Strategy project charter is created in which Chatbots Strategy project management process group?

78. To what extent has the intervention strategy been adapted to the areas of intervention in which it is being implemented?

79. Will the products created live up to the necessary quality?

80. If a risk event occurs, what will you do?

81. First of all, should any action be taken?

82. What input will you be required to provide the Chatbots Strategy project team?

83. Did the program design/ implementation strategy adequately address the planning stage necessary to set up structures, hire staff etc.?

84. To what extent do the intervention objectives and strategies of the Chatbots Strategy project respond to your organizations plans?

85. Professionals want to know what is expected from them; what are the deliverables?

86. You did your readings, yes?

87. How will you do it?

88. In what ways can the governance of the Chatbots Strategy project be improved so that it has greater likelihood of achieving future sustainability?

89. What should you do next?

90. How well do the team follow the chosen processes?

91. What factors are contributing to progress or delay in the achievement of products and results?

92. If you are late, will anybody notice?

2.1 Project Management Plan: Chatbots Strategy

93. Is the budget realistic?

94. Are there any scope changes proposed for a previously authorized Chatbots Strategy project?

95. Does the implementation plan have an appropriate division of responsibilities?

96. What should you drop in order to add something new?

97. Development trends and opportunities. What if the positive direction and vision of your organization causes expected trends to change?

98. Do there need to be organizational changes?

99. Where does all this information come from?

100. How do you manage integration?

101. Are the proposed Chatbots Strategy project purposes different than a previously authorized Chatbots Strategy project?

102. Are comparable cost estimates used for comparing, screening and selecting alternative plans, and has a reasonable cost estimate been developed for the recommended plan?

103. What data/reports/tools/etc. do your PMs need?

104. Is there anything you would now do differently on your Chatbots Strategy project based on past experience?

105. What went wrong?

106. What is the justification?

107. Is mitigation authorized or recommended?

108. What are the known stakeholder requirements?

109. What goes into your Chatbots Strategy project Charter?

2.2 Scope Management Plan: Chatbots Strategy

110. Are actuals compared against estimates to analyze and correct variances?

111. Do you have funding for Chatbots Strategy project and product development, implementation and on-going support?

112. Sensitivity analysis?

113. Can the Chatbots Strategy project team do several activities in parallel?

114. Has a structured approach been used to break work effort into manageable components (WBS)?

115. Does a documented Chatbots Strategy project organizational policy & plan (i.e. governance model) exist?

116. What are the risks of not having good inter-organization cooperation on the Chatbots Strategy project?

117. Where do scope processes fit in?

118. When is corrective or preventative action required?

119. What happens to rejected deliverables?

120. Do Chatbots Strategy project managers participating in the Chatbots Strategy project know the Chatbots Strategy projects true status first hand?

121. How difficult will it be to do specific activities on this Chatbots Strategy project?

122. What are the risks that could significantly affect the resources needed for the Chatbots Strategy project?

123. Are calculations and results of analyzes essentially correct?

124. Are metrics used to evaluate and manage Vendors?

125. Are software metrics formally captured, analyzed and used as a basis for other Chatbots Strategy project estimates?

126. Have Chatbots Strategy project team accountabilities & responsibilities been clearly defined?

127. Is each item clearly and completely defined?

128. Are the existing and future without-plan conditions reasonable and appropriate?

129. Were Chatbots Strategy project team members involved in detailed estimating and scheduling?

2.3 Requirements Management Plan: Chatbots Strategy

130. After the requirements are gathered and set forth on the requirements register, theyre little more than a laundry list of items. Some may be duplicates, some might conflict with others and some will be too broad or too vague to understand. Describe how the requirements will be analyzed. Who will perform the analysis?

131. Is the system software (non-operating system) new to the IT Chatbots Strategy project team?

132. Is requirements work dependent on any other specific Chatbots Strategy project or non-Chatbots Strategy project activities (e.g. funding, approvals, procurement)?

133. Have stakeholders been instructed in the Change Control process?

134. Who will do the reporting and to whom will reports be delivered?

135. Did you avoid subjective, flowery or non-specific statements?

136. Do you have an agreed upon process for alerting the Chatbots Strategy project Manager if a request for change in requirements leads to a product scope change?

137. Did you provide clear and concise specifications?

138. Who is responsible for monitoring and tracking the Chatbots Strategy project requirements?

139. Do you understand the role that each stakeholder will play in the requirements process?

140. How will unresolved questions be handled once approval has been obtained?

141. How will you develop the schedule of requirements activities?

142. What performance metrics will be used?

143. In case of software development; Should you have a test for each code module?

144. Who will initially review the Chatbots Strategy project work or products to ensure it meets the applicable acceptance criteria?

145. Do you have an appropriate arrangement for meetings?

146. What cost metrics will be used?

147. What is the earliest finish date for this Chatbots Strategy project if it is scheduled to start on ...?

148. Will the contractors involved take full responsibility?

149. Why manage requirements?

2.4 Requirements Documentation: Chatbots Strategy

150. The problem with gathering requirements is right there in the word gathering. What images does it conjure?

151. What are the acceptance criteria?

152. How much does requirements engineering cost?

153. Can the requirements be checked?

154. Where are business rules being captured?

155. Is the requirement properly understood?

156. Consistency. are there any requirements conflicts?

157. How does what is being described meet the business need?

158. Who provides requirements?

159. What is a show stopper in the requirements?

160. What is effective documentation?

161. Are all functions required by the customer included?

162. What are the attributes of a customer?

163. How linear / iterative is your Requirements Gathering process (or will it be)?

164. Are there any requirements conflicts?

165. What marketing channels do you want to use: e-mail, letter or sms?

166. How can you document system requirements?

167. What images does it conjure?

168. How to document system requirements?

169. What is your Elevator Speech?

2.5 Requirements Traceability Matrix: Chatbots Strategy

170. Do you have a clear understanding of all subcontracts in place?

171. Describe the process for approving requirements so they can be added to the traceability matrix and Chatbots Strategy project work can be performed. Will the Chatbots Strategy project requirements become approved in writing?

172. Will you use a Requirements Traceability Matrix?

173. What are the chronologies, contingencies, consequences, criteria?

174. Why do you manage scope?

175. How do you manage scope?

176. What is the WBS?

177. What percentage of Chatbots Strategy projects are producing traceability matrices between requirements and other work products?

178. How will it affect the stakeholders personally in career?

179. Why use a WBS?

180. How small is small enough?

181. Is there a requirements traceability process in place?

2.6 Project Scope Statement: Chatbots Strategy

182. Is there an information system for the Chatbots Strategy project?

183. What went right?

184. If there are vendors, have they signed off on the Chatbots Strategy project Plan?

185. Chatbots Strategy project lead, team lead, solution architect?

186. Are there completion/verification criteria defined for each task producing an output?

187. What process would you recommend for creating the Chatbots Strategy project scope statement?

188. Will the risk plan be updated on a regular and frequent basis?

189. Is the Chatbots Strategy project sponsor function identified and defined?

190. Elements of scope management that deal with concept development ?

191. Identify how your team and you will create the Chatbots Strategy project scope statement and the work breakdown structure (WBS). Document how you will create the Chatbots Strategy project scope

statement and WBS, and make sure you answer the following questions: In defining Chatbots Strategy project scope and the WBS, will you and your Chatbots Strategy project team be using methods defined by your organization, methods defined by the Chatbots Strategy project management office (PMO), or other methods?

192. Were potential customers involved early in the planning process?

193. Is the Chatbots Strategy project manager qualified and experienced in Chatbots Strategy project management?

194. Where and how does the team fit within your organization structure?

195. Is the quality function identified and assigned?

196. Will you need a statement of work?

197. Will the risk status be reported to management on a regular and frequent basis?

198. Once its defined, what is the stability of the Chatbots Strategy project scope?

199. Any new risks introduced or old risks impacted. Are there issues that could affect the existing requirements for the result, service, or product if the scope changes?

200. If you were to write a list of what should not be included in the scope statement, what are the things that you would recommend be described as out-of-

scope?

2.7 Assumption and Constraint Log: Chatbots Strategy

201. Can you perform this task or activity in a more effective manner?

202. Are there procedures in place to effectively manage interdependencies with other Chatbots Strategy projects / systems?

203. Is there adequate stakeholder participation for the vetting of requirements definition, changes and management?

204. Does a specific action and/or state that is known to violate security policy occur?

205. Is the process working, and people are not executing in compliance of the process?

206. What if failure during recovery?

207. What weaknesses do you have?

208. Was the document/deliverable developed per the appropriate or required standards (for example, Institute of Electrical and Electronics Engineers standards)?

209. When can log be discarded?

210. Is this process still needed?

211. Security analysis has access to information that is sanitized?

212. What strengths do you have?

213. If it is out of compliance, should the process be amended or should the Plan be amended?

214. Are there ways to reduce the time it takes to get something approved?

215. What do you log?

216. If appropriate, is the deliverable content consistent with current Chatbots Strategy project documents and in compliance with the Document Management Plan?

217. What does an audit system look like?

218. Are best practices and metrics employed to identify issues, progress, performance, etc.?

219. Have all involved stakeholders and work groups committed to the Chatbots Strategy project?

220. Are there nonconformance issues?

2.8 Work Breakdown Structure: Chatbots Strategy

221. Is the work breakdown structure (wbs) defined and is the scope of the Chatbots Strategy project clear with assigned deliverable owners?

222. What has to be done?

223. Why would you develop a Work Breakdown Structure?

224. How far down?

225. When do you stop?

226. How big is a work-package?

227. When does it have to be done?

228. Can you make it?

229. How will you and your Chatbots Strategy project team define the Chatbots Strategy projects scope and work breakdown structure?

230. Is it still viable?

231. How much detail?

232. Do you need another level?

233. Why is it useful?

234. What is the probability of completing the Chatbots Strategy project in less that xx days?

235. Where does it take place?

236. When would you develop a Work Breakdown Structure?

237. How many levels?

2.9 WBS Dictionary: Chatbots Strategy

238. Budgeted cost for work performed?

239. Are your organizations and items of cost assigned to each pool identified?

240. Is undistributed budget limited to contract effort which cannot yet be planned to CWBS elements at or below the level specified for reporting to the Government?

241. Identify potential or actual budget-based and time-based schedule variances?

242. Are the requirements for all items of overhead established by rational, traceable processes?

243. Are retroactive changes to budgets for completed work specifically prohibited in an established procedure, and is this procedure adhered to?

244. What is wrong with this Chatbots Strategy project?

245. Does the scheduling system provide for the identification of work progress against technical and other milestones, and also provide for forecasts of completion dates of scheduled work?

246. Is authorization of budgets in excess of the

contract budget base controlled formally and done with the full knowledge and recognition of the procuring activity?

247. Is all contract work included in the CWBS?

248. Does the contractors system provide unit or lot costs when applicable?

249. Are time-phased budgets established for planning and control of level of effort activity by category of resource; for example, type of manpower and/or material?

250. Are estimates of costs at completion utilized in determining contract funding requirements and reporting them?

251. Are significant decision points, constraints, and interfaces identified as key milestones?

252. Are work packages reasonably short in time duration or do they have adequate objective indicators/milestones to minimize subjectivity of the in process work evaluation?

253. Are all affected work authorizations, budgeting, and scheduling documents amended to properly reflect the effects of authorized changes?

2.10 Schedule Management Plan: Chatbots Strategy

254. What threats might prevent you from getting there?

255. Is the development plan and/or process documented?

256. Is there anything planned that does not need to be here?

257. Perform reality checks on schedules – are all tasks included?

258. Is your organization certified as a broker of the products/supplies?

259. Are any non-compliance issues that exist due to your organizations practices communicated to your organization?

260. Is there a formal set of procedures supporting Issues Management?

261. Have Chatbots Strategy project management standards and procedures been identified / established and documented?

262. Are the key elements of a Chatbots Strategy project Charter present?

263. Does all Chatbots Strategy project

documentation reside in a common repository for easy access?

264. Can additional resources be added to subsequent tasks to reduce the durations of the already stated tasks?

265. Are vendor contract reports, reviews and visits conducted periodically?

266. Are assumptions being identified, recorded, analyzed, qualified and closed?

267. Are the activity durations realistic and at an appropriate level of detail for effective management?

268. Is there a requirements change management processes in place?

269. Has process improvement efforts been completed before requirements efforts begin?

270. Has the scope management document been updated and distributed to help prevent scope creep?

271. Have Chatbots Strategy project team accountabilities & responsibilities been clearly defined?

272. Is the ims used by all levels of management for Chatbots Strategy project implementation and control?

2.11 Activity List: Chatbots Strategy

273. What went well?

274. How can the Chatbots Strategy project be displayed graphically to better visualize the activities?

275. What is your organizations history in doing similar activities?

276. Is infrastructure setup part of your Chatbots Strategy project?

277. What did not go as well?

278. What is the total time required to complete the Chatbots Strategy project if no delays occur?

279. How much slack is available in the Chatbots Strategy project?

280. How should ongoing costs be monitored to try to keep the Chatbots Strategy project within budget?

281. Should you include sub-activities?

282. What will be performed?

283. How will it be performed?

284. The wbs is developed as part of a joint planning session. and how do you know that youhave done this right?

285. Are the required resources available or need to be acquired?

286. When will the work be performed?

287. For other activities, how much delay can be tolerated?

288. Who will perform the work?

289. What is the LF and LS for each activity?

290. What are the critical bottleneck activities?

291. When do the individual activities need to start and finish?

2.12 Activity Attributes: Chatbots Strategy

292. How many days do you need to complete the work scope with a limit of X number of resources?

293. How else could the items be grouped?

294. Resource is assigned to?

295. How difficult will it be to do specific activities on this Chatbots Strategy project?

296. Can you re-assign any activities to another resource to resolve an over-allocation?

297. Is there a trend during the year?

298. What is the general pattern here?

299. Has management defined a definite timeframe for the turnaround or Chatbots Strategy project window?

300. Resources to accomplish the work?

301. What activity do you think you should spend the most time on?

302. Why?

303. Have constraints been applied to the start and finish milestones for the phases?

304. What conclusions/generalizations can you draw from this?

305. Do you feel very comfortable with your prediction?

306. How difficult will it be to complete specific activities on this Chatbots Strategy project?

307. Time for overtime?

308. Which method produces the more accurate cost assignment?

2.13 Milestone List: Chatbots Strategy

309. Identify critical paths (one or more) and which activities are on the critical path?

310. Can you derive how soon can the whole Chatbots Strategy project finish?

311. Usps (unique selling points)?

312. How do you manage time?

313. Information and research?

314. Loss of key staff?

315. Continuity, supply chain robustness?

316. Political effects?

317. Effects on core activities, distraction?

318. Sustainable financial backing?

319. What is the market for your technology, product or service?

320. What would happen if a delivery of material was one week late?

321. Do you foresee any technical risks or developmental challenges?

322. How soon can the activity start?

323. When will the Chatbots Strategy project be complete?

324. What specific improvements did you make to the Chatbots Strategy project proposal since the previous time?

325. How difficult will it be to do specific activities on this Chatbots Strategy project?

326. What background experience, skills, and strengths does the team bring to your organization?

327. What are your competitors vulnerabilities?

2.14 Network Diagram: Chatbots Strategy

328. Where do you schedule uncertainty time?

329. What is the completion time?

330. Exercise: what is the probability that the Chatbots Strategy project duration will exceed xx weeks?

331. Are you on time?

332. Planning: who, how long, what to do?

333. Which type of network diagram allows you to depict four types of dependencies?

334. What job or jobs follow it?

335. Where do schedules come from?

336. What is the probability of completing the Chatbots Strategy project in less that xx days?

337. If a current contract exists, can you provide the vendor name, contract start, and contract expiration date?

338. What are the Key Success Factors?

339. What activity must be completed immediately before this activity can start?

340. How difficult will it be to do specific activities on this Chatbots Strategy project?

341. How confident can you be in your milestone dates and the delivery date?

342. What are the Major Administrative Issues?

343. Will crashing x weeks return more in benefits than it costs?

344. What job or jobs precede it?

345. What controls the start and finish of a job?

346. Why must you schedule milestones, such as reviews, throughout the Chatbots Strategy project?

347. What job or jobs could run concurrently?

2.15 Activity Resource Requirements: Chatbots Strategy

348. Organizational Applicability?

349. What is the Work Plan Standard?

350. Why do you do that?

351. What are constraints that you might find during the Human Resource Planning process?

352. Do you use tools like decomposition and rolling-wave planning to produce the activity list and other outputs?

353. Anything else?

354. How many signatures do you require on a check and does this match what is in your policy and procedures?

355. Which logical relationship does the PDM use most often?

356. Other support in specific areas?

357. Are there unresolved issues that need to be addressed?

358. When does monitoring begin?

359. How do you handle petty cash?

2.16 Resource Breakdown Structure: Chatbots Strategy

360. How should the information be delivered?

361. Changes based on input from stakeholders?

362. What is the primary purpose of the human resource plan?

363. Is predictive resource analysis being done?

364. Which resources should be in the resource pool?

365. What is Chatbots Strategy project communication management?

366. What can you do to improve productivity?

367. What is the number one predictor of a groups productivity?

368. What are the requirements for resource data?

369. Why time management?

370. Goals for the Chatbots Strategy project. What is each stakeholders desired outcome for the Chatbots Strategy project?

371. When do they need the information?

372. Who is allowed to perform which functions?

373. Who is allowed to see what data about which resources?

374. What defines a successful Chatbots Strategy project?

375. Who will use the system?

2.17 Activity Duration Estimates: Chatbots Strategy

376. Are costs that may be needed to account for Chatbots Strategy project risks determined?

377. Why is it important to determine activity sequencing on Chatbots Strategy projects?

378. Do procedures exist describing how the Chatbots Strategy project scope will be managed?

379. What is the difference between conceptual, application, and evaluative questions?

380. Which best describes how this affects the Chatbots Strategy project?

381. Will additional funds be needed for hardware or software?

382. When a risk event occurs, is the risk response evaluated and the appropriate response implemented?

383. Does a process exist to determine which risk events to accept and which events to disregard?

384. Why do you think schedule issues often cause the most conflicts on Chatbots Strategy projects?

385. Could it have been avoided?

386. What is the shortest possible time it will take to complete this Chatbots Strategy project?

387. What are two suggestions for ensuring adequate change control on Chatbots Strategy projects that involve outside contracts?

388. Are expert judgment and historical information utilized to estimate activity duration?

389. Calculate the expected duration for an activity that has a most likely time of 5, a pessimistic time of 13, and a optimiztic time of 3?

390. Who will provide inputs for it?

391. Is corrective action taken to bring Chatbots Strategy project performance into line with the Chatbots Strategy project plan?

392. Which frame seemed to be the most important and why?

393. Do scope statements include the Chatbots Strategy project objectives and expected deliverables?

2.18 Duration Estimating Worksheet: Chatbots Strategy

394. How should ongoing costs be monitored to try to keep the Chatbots Strategy project within budget?

395. What info is needed?

396. Value pocket identification & quantification what are value pockets?

397. Science = process: remember the scientific method?

398. How can the Chatbots Strategy project be displayed graphically to better visualize the activities?

399. Small or large Chatbots Strategy project?

400. When, then?

401. Is this operation cost effective?

402. What questions do you have?

403. Is a construction detail attached (to aid in explanation)?

404. Can the Chatbots Strategy project be constructed as planned?

405. Will the Chatbots Strategy project collaborate with the local community and leverage resources?

406. What is next?

407. What is your role?

408. What utility impacts are there?

409. Do any colleagues have experience with your organization and/or RFPs?

2.19 Project Schedule: Chatbots Strategy

410. Meet requirements?

411. Are all remaining durations correct?

412. Does the condition or event threaten the Chatbots Strategy projects objectives in any ways?

413. Your Chatbots Strategy project management plan results in a Chatbots Strategy project schedule that is too long. If the Chatbots Strategy project network diagram cannot change and you have extra personnel resources, what is the BEST thing to do?

414. How effectively were issues able to be resolved without impacting the Chatbots Strategy project Schedule or Budget?

415. How can you minimize or control changes to Chatbots Strategy project schedules?

416. Master Chatbots Strategy project schedule?

417. How do you manage Chatbots Strategy project Risk?

418. What is risk management?

419. Was the Chatbots Strategy project schedule reviewed by all stakeholders and formally accepted?

420. Why or why not?

421. Are quality inspections and review activities listed in the Chatbots Strategy project schedule(s)?

422. If you can not fix it, how do you do it differently?

423. What is risk?

424. How much slack is available in the Chatbots Strategy project?

425. What is the purpose of a Chatbots Strategy project schedule?

426. Are procedures defined by which the Chatbots Strategy project schedule may be changed?

427. Should you have a test for each code module?

2.20 Cost Management Plan: Chatbots Strategy

428. Is stakeholder involvement adequate?

429. Risk Analysis?

430. Is there general agreement & acceptance of the current status and progress of the Chatbots Strategy project?

431. Are decisions captured in a decisions log?

432. Contractors scope – how will contractors scope be defined when contracts are let?

433. Have all necessary approvals been obtained?

434. Cost variances – how will cost variances be identified and corrected?

435. How relevant is this attribute to this Chatbots Strategy project or audit?

436. Are Chatbots Strategy project team members committed fulltime?

437. Does the business case include how the Chatbots Strategy project aligns with your organizations strategic goals & objectives?

438. Have the procedures for identifying budget variances been followed?

439. Is there a Steering Committee in place?

440. Has your organization readiness assessment been conducted?

441. Has the budget been baselined?

442. Have all documents been archived in a Chatbots Strategy project repository for each release?

443. How difficult will it be to do specific tasks on the Chatbots Strategy project?

444. What is your organizations history in doing similar tasks?

445. Is there a formal set of procedures supporting Stakeholder Management?

2.21 Activity Cost Estimates: Chatbots Strategy

446. Are data needed on characteristics of care?

447. Maintenance Reserve?

448. What are you looking for?

449. Does the activity rely on a common set of tools to carry it out?

450. What were things that you need to improve?

451. Estimated cost?

452. How do you fund change orders?

453. What is the activity inventory?

454. What is the activity recast of the budget?

455. What communication items need improvement?

456. If you are asked to lower your estimate because the price is too high, what are your options?

457. What makes a good activity description?

458. Will you use any tools, such as Chatbots Strategy project management software, to assist in capturing Earned Value metrics?

459. Measurable - are the targets measurable?

460. What areas does the group agree are the biggest success on the Chatbots Strategy project?

461. What makes a good expected result statement?

462. How do you allocate indirect costs to activities?

463. What cost data should be used to estimate costs during the 2-year follow-up period?

464. Vac -variance at completion, how much over/ under budget do you expect to be?

2.22 Cost Estimating Worksheet: Chatbots Strategy

465. Ask: are others positioned to know, are others credible, and will others cooperate?

466. How will the results be shared and to whom?

467. What can be included?

468. Identify the timeframe necessary to monitor progress and collect data to determine how the selected measure has changed?

469. What will others want?

470. What is the estimated labor cost today based upon this information?

471. Will the Chatbots Strategy project collaborate with the local community and leverage resources?

472. What additional Chatbots Strategy project(s) could be initiated as a result of this Chatbots Strategy project?

473. Does the Chatbots Strategy project provide innovative ways for stakeholders to overcome obstacles or deliver better outcomes?

474. What happens to any remaining funds not used?

475. Is the Chatbots Strategy project responsive to

community need?

476. Is it feasible to establish a control group arrangement?

477. Can a trend be established from historical performance data on the selected measure and are the criteria for using trend analysis or forecasting methods met?

478. What costs are to be estimated?

479. Who is best positioned to know and assist in identifying corresponding factors?

480. What is the purpose of estimating?

2.23 Cost Baseline: Chatbots Strategy

481. How concrete were original objectives?

482. What is the consequence?

483. Will the Chatbots Strategy project fail if the change request is not executed?

484. Is there anything unique in this Chatbots Strategy projects scope statement that will affect resources?

485. Has operations management formally accepted responsibility for operating and maintaining the product(s) or service(s) delivered by the Chatbots Strategy project?

486. Have the resources used by the Chatbots Strategy project been reassigned to other units or Chatbots Strategy projects?

487. At which frequency ?

488. How will cost estimates be used?

489. On budget?

490. What does a good WBS NOT look like?

491. Does a process exist for establishing a cost baseline to measure Chatbots Strategy project performance?

492. Does the suggested change request represent a

desired enhancement to the products functionality?

493. Where do changes come from?

494. Have the actual milestone completion dates been compared to the approved schedule?

495. Are you meeting with your team regularly?

496. How likely is it to go wrong?

497. Has the Chatbots Strategy project (or Chatbots Strategy project phase) been evaluated against each objective established in the product description and Integrated Chatbots Strategy project Plan?

498. For what purpose ?

2.24 Quality Management Plan: Chatbots Strategy

499. How are calibration records kept?

500. How does your organization manage work to promote cooperation, individual initiative, innovation, flexibility, communications, and knowledge/skill sharing across work units?

501. Was trending evident between audits?

502. How is the information recorded?

503. Does the plan conform to standards?

504. How does your organization design processes to ensure others meet customer and others requirements?

505. Is there a procedure for this process?

506. What are the established criteria that sampling / testing data are compared against?

507. How does your organization decide what to measure?

508. Is this a Requirement?

509. How does your organization manage training and evaluate its effectiveness?

510. Show/provide copy of procedures for taking field notes?

511. What key performance indicators does your organization use to measure, manage, and improve key processes?

512. Do trained quality assurance auditors conduct the audits as defined in the Quality Management Plan and scheduled by the Chatbots Strategy project manager?

513. What data do you gather/use/compile?

514. Who is responsible?

515. How are changes approved?

516. What is quality planning ?

517. What procedures are used to determine if you use, and the number of split, replicate or duplicate samples taken at a site?

2.25 Quality Metrics: Chatbots Strategy

518. What happens if you get an abnormal result?

519. What if the biggest risk to your business were the already stated people who do not complain?

520. What documentation is required?

521. Where is quality now?

522. Was the overall quality better or worse than previous products?

523. How can the effectiveness of each of the activities be measured?

524. Is quality culture a competitive advantage?

525. What percentage are outcome-based?

526. Can visual measures help you to filter visualizations of interest?

527. Are quality metrics defined?

528. Are documents on hand to provide explanations of privacy and confidentiality?

529. Were number of defects identified?

530. What does this tell us?

531. Where did complaints, returns and warranty claims come from?

532. When will the Final Guidance will be issued?

533. Do you know how much profit a 10% decrease in waste would generate?

534. What metrics do you measure?

535. What level of statistical confidence do you use?

536. Do the operators focus on determining; is there anything you need to worry about?

537. Subjective quality component: customer satisfaction, how do you measure it?

2.26 Process Improvement Plan: Chatbots Strategy

538. Where do you want to be?

539. Are there forms and procedures to collect and record the data?

540. Why quality management?

541. Has a process guide to collect the data been developed?

542. Purpose of goal: the motive is determined by asking, why do you want to achieve this goal?

543. What personnel are the coaches for your initiative?

544. What personnel are the champions for the initiative?

545. Have the supporting tools been developed or acquired?

546. Does your process ensure quality?

547. Modeling current processes is great, and will you ever see a return on that investment?

548. Are you making progress on the goals?

549. The motive is determined by asking, Why do you

want to achieve this goal?

550. Are you making progress on your improvement plan?

551. Who should prepare the process improvement action plan?

552. Has the time line required to move measurement results from the points of collection to databases or users been established?

553. Management commitment at all levels?

554. Why do you want to achieve the goal?

555. Everyone agrees on what process improvement is, right?

2.27 Responsibility Assignment Matrix: Chatbots Strategy

556. How many hours by each staff member/rate?

557. What do you do when people do not respond?

558. What travel needed?

559. Budgeted cost for work scheduled?

560. All cwbs elements specified for external reporting?

561. The anticipated business volume?

562. The already stated responsible for overhead performance control of related costs?

563. When performing is split among two or more roles, is the work clearly defined so that the efforts are coordinated and the communication is clear?

564. Are all authorized tasks assigned to identified organizational elements?

565. What will the work cost?

566. Are overhead costs budgets established on a basis consistent with anticipated direct business base?

567. The staff characteristics – is the group or the

person capable to work together as a team?

568. Are the bases and rates for allocating costs from each indirect pool consistently applied?

569. With too many people labeled as doing the work, are there too many hands involved?

570. Are estimates of costs at completion generated in a rational, consistent manner?

571. Undistributed budgets, if any?

572. Do others have the time to dedicate to your Chatbots Strategy project?

573. Will too many Signing-off responsibilities delay the completion of the activity/deliverable?

2.28 Roles and Responsibilities: Chatbots Strategy

574. Do you take the time to clearly define roles and responsibilities on Chatbots Strategy project tasks?

575. Do the values and practices inherent in the culture of your organization foster or hinder the process?

576. Are Chatbots Strategy project team roles and responsibilities identified and documented?

577. Attainable / achievable: the goal is attainable; can you actually accomplish the goal?

578. How well did the Chatbots Strategy project Team understand the expectations of specific roles and responsibilities?

579. Be specific; avoid generalities. Thank you and great work alone are insufficient. What exactly do you appreciate and why?

580. Influence: what areas of organizational decision making are you able to influence when you do not have authority to make the final decision?

581. Are the quality assurance functions and related roles and responsibilities clearly defined?

582. What expectations were met?

583. Once the responsibilities are defined for the Chatbots Strategy project, have the deliverables, roles and responsibilities been clearly communicated to every participant?

584. What should you do now to prepare yourself for a promotion, increased responsibilities or a different job?

585. Authority: what areas/Chatbots Strategy projects in your work do you have the authority to decide upon and act on the already stated decisions?

586. Is feedback clearly communicated and non-judgmental?

587. What should you highlight for improvement?

588. Are governance roles and responsibilities documented?

589. What should you do now to ensure that you are meeting all expectations of your current position?

590. How is your work-life balance?

591. To decide whether to use a quality measurement, ask how will you know when it is achieved?

592. Accountabilities: what are the roles and responsibilities of individual team members?

2.29 Human Resource Management Plan: Chatbots Strategy

593. What is the boss?

594. Is this Chatbots Strategy project carried out in partnership with other groups/organizations?

595. Do all stakeholders know how to access this repository and where to find the Chatbots Strategy project documentation?

596. Are software metrics formally captured, analyzed and used as a basis for other Chatbots Strategy project estimates?

597. How do you determine what key skills and talents are needed to meet the objectives. Is your organization primarily focused on a specific industry?

598. Based on your Chatbots Strategy project communication management plan, what worked well?

599. Have reserves been created to address risks?

600. Have Chatbots Strategy project team accountabilities & responsibilities been clearly defined?

601. Were decisions made in a timely manner?

602. Are vendor invoices audited for accuracy before

payment?

603. Is there a Quality Management Plan?

604. Is documentation created for communication with the suppliers and Vendors?

605. Are meeting minutes captured and sent out after the meeting?

606. Have Chatbots Strategy project management standards and procedures been identified / established and documented?

607. Are Chatbots Strategy project team members committed fulltime?

608. Does the Chatbots Strategy project have a Quality Culture?

609. Do you have the reasons why the changes to your organizational systems and capabilities are required?

610. Has a provision been made to reassess Chatbots Strategy project risks at various Chatbots Strategy project stages?

2.30 Communications Management Plan: Chatbots Strategy

611. Why manage stakeholders?

612. Is the stakeholder role recognized by your organization?

613. Will messages be directly related to the release strategy or phases of the Chatbots Strategy project?

614. Who did you turn to if you had questions?

615. Do you have members of your team responsible for certain stakeholders?

616. Who is the stakeholder?

617. What to know?

618. Are the stakeholders getting the information others need, are others consulted, are concerns addressed?

619. What communications method?

620. Who to learn from?

621. What is the stakeholders level of authority?

622. Who to share with?

623. Are stakeholders internal or external?

624. What approaches do you use?

625. How did the term stakeholder originate?

626. How often do you engage with stakeholders?

627. Are there potential barriers between the team and the stakeholder?

628. Who are the members of the governing body?

2.31 Risk Management Plan: Chatbots Strategy

629. Risk categories: what are the main categories of risks that should be addressed on this Chatbots Strategy project?

630. Do you train all developers in the process?

631. Where are you confronted with risks during the business phases?

632. Market risk -will the new service or product be useful to your organization or marketable to others?

633. How quickly does this item need to be resolved?

634. Are there new risks that mitigation strategies might introduce?

635. Do you have a consistent repeatable process that is actually used?

636. Are status updates being made on schedule and are the updates clearly described?

637. What will drive change?

638. What is the likelihood?

639. What does a risk management program do?

640. What should be done with non-critical risks?

641. Workarounds are determined during which step of risk management?

642. Are requirements fully understood by the software engineering team and customers?

643. User involvement: do you have the right users?

644. Financial risk -can your organization afford to undertake the Chatbots Strategy project?

645. Why might it be late?

646. What things might go wrong?

647. Internal technical and management reviews?

2.32 Risk Register: Chatbots Strategy

648. Are there any knock-on effects/impact on any of the other areas?

649. When is it going to be done?

650. Technology risk -is the Chatbots Strategy project technically feasible?

651. When will it happen?

652. Amongst the action plans and recommendations that you have to introduce are there some that could stop or delay the overall program?

653. Preventative actions - planned actions to reduce the likelihood a risk will occur and/or reduce the seriousness should it occur. What should you do now?

654. How are risks identified?

655. People risk -are people with appropriate skills available to help complete the Chatbots Strategy project?

656. Risk documentation: what reporting formats and processes will be used for risk management activities?

657. What should you do when?

658. Financial risk -can your organization afford to undertake the Chatbots Strategy project?

659. Manageability – have mitigations to the risk been identified?

660. How often will the Risk Management Plan and Risk Register be formally reviewed, and by whom?

661. Can the likelihood and impact of failing to achieve corresponding recommendations and action plans be assessed?

662. Cost/benefit – how much will the proposed mitigations cost and how does this cost compare with the potential cost of the risk event/situation should it occur?

663. What has changed since the last period?

664. What should the audit role be in establishing a risk management process?

665. Does the evidence highlight any areas to advance opportunities or foster good relations. If yes what steps will be taken?

666. What are the major risks facing the Chatbots Strategy project?

2.33 Probability and Impact Assessment: Chatbots Strategy

667. What are the levels of understanding of the future users of the outcome/results of this Chatbots Strategy project?

668. What risks does your organization have if the Chatbots Strategy projects fail to meet deadline?

669. Are testing tools available and suitable?

670. What are your data sources?

671. Is the technology to be built new to your organization?

672. What are the uncertainties associated with the technology selected for the Chatbots Strategy project?

673. What are the risks involved in appointing external agencies to manage the Chatbots Strategy project?

674. Are enough people available?

675. Which risks need to move on to Perform Quantitative Risk Analysis?

676. Risk urgency assessment -which of your risks could occur soon, or require a longer planning time?

677. Can this technology be absorbed with current

level of expertise available in your organization?

678. How solid is the Chatbots Strategy projection of competitive reaction?

679. Who has experience with this?

680. How is risk handled within this Chatbots Strategy project organization?

681. Risks should be identified during which phase of Chatbots Strategy project management life cycle?

682. Assumptions analysis -what assumptions have you made or been given about your Chatbots Strategy project?

683. Costs associated with late delivery or a defective product?

2.34 Probability and Impact Matrix: Chatbots Strategy

684. What action would you take to the identified risks in the Chatbots Strategy project?

685. What should be done NEXT?

686. Mandated specific features?

687. Brain storm – mind maps, what if?

688. What is your anticipated volatility of the requirements?

689. How likely is the current plan to come in on schedule or on budget?

690. How to prioritize risks?

691. Are flexibility and reuse paramount?

692. Have top software and customer managers formally committed to support the Chatbots Strategy project?

693. How will economic events and trends likely affect the Chatbots Strategy project?

694. Are the risk data timely and relevant?

695. Can you avoid altogether some things that might go wrong?

696. What are the ways you measure and evaluate risks?

697. How is the risk management process used in practice?

698. Have staff received necessary training?

699. Is a software Chatbots Strategy project management tool available?

700. Pay attention to the quality of the plans: is the content complete, or does it seem to be lacking detail?

701. During Chatbots Strategy project executing, a team member identifies a risk that is not in the risk register. What should you do?

702. How do you analyze the risks in the different types of Chatbots Strategy projects?

703. During which risk management process is a determination to transfer a risk made?

2.35 Risk Data Sheet: Chatbots Strategy

704. How can hazards be reduced?

705. Do effective diagnostic tests exist?

706. How do you handle product safely?

707. Who has a vested interest in how you perform as your organization (our stakeholders)?

708. Whom do you serve (customers)?

709. What can happen?

710. Type of risk identified?

711. What are you trying to achieve (Objectives)?

712. Has a sensitivity analysis been carried out?

713. What if client refuses?

714. What are the main threats to your existence?

715. Are new hazards created?

716. Potential for recurrence?

717. What were the Causes that contributed?

718. What are your core values?

719. Will revised controls lead to tolerable risk levels?

720. What are you weak at and therefore need to do better?

721. Has the most cost-effective solution been chosen?

2.36 Procurement Management Plan: Chatbots Strategy

722. Why do you do it?

723. Are enough systems & user personnel assigned to the Chatbots Strategy project?

724. Pareto diagrams, statistical sampling, flow charting or trend analysis used quality monitoring?

725. Are non-critical path items updated and agreed upon with the teams?

726. Is it possible to track all classes of Chatbots Strategy project work (e.g. scheduled, un-scheduled, defect repair, etc.)?

727. Is there an issues management plan in place?

728. Was the Chatbots Strategy project schedule reviewed by all stakeholders and formally accepted?

729. Have Chatbots Strategy project team accountabilities & responsibilities been clearly defined?

730. Does the resource management plan include a personnel development plan?

731. Are the schedule estimates reasonable given the Chatbots Strategy project?

732. Does the Chatbots Strategy project have a Quality Culture?

733. If independent estimates will be needed as evaluation criteria, who will prepare them and when?

734. Has the schedule been baselined?

735. Financial capacity; does the seller have, or can the seller reasonably be expected to obtain, the financial resources needed?

736. Is pert / critical path or equivalent methodology being used?

737. Is there a procurement management plan in place?

738. Do Chatbots Strategy project managers participating in the Chatbots Strategy project know the Chatbots Strategy projects true status first hand?

739. Are key risk mitigation strategies added to the Chatbots Strategy project schedule?

2.37 Source Selection Criteria: Chatbots Strategy

740. What is the effect of the debriefing schedule on potential protests?

741. What common questions or problems are associated with debriefings?

742. How important is cost in the source selection decision relative to past performance and technical considerations?

743. Can you make a cost/technical tradeoff?

744. What management structure does your organization consider as optimal for performing the contract?

745. What benefits are accrued from issuing a DRFP in advance of issuing a final RFP?

746. What are open book debriefings?

747. What should be considered when developing evaluation standards?

748. How should oral presentations be prepared for?

749. How much weight should be placed on past performance information?

750. What is the role of counsel in the procurement

process?

751. Is there collaboration among your evaluators?

752. What can not be disclosed?

753. Does your documentation identify why the team concurs or differs with reported performance from past performance report (CPARs, questionnaire responses, etc.)?

754. Is the contracting office likely to receive more purchase requests for this item or service during the coming year?

755. How should the oral presentations be handled?

756. What should be the contracting officers strategy?

757. What are the special considerations for preaward debriefings?

758. How can the methods of publicizing the buy be tailored to yield more effective price competition?

759. How much past performance information should be requested?

2.38 Stakeholder Management Plan: Chatbots Strategy

760. Are adequate resources provided for the quality assurance function?

761. Have all stakeholders been identified?

762. Has a capability assessment been conducted?

763. Are action items captured and managed?

764. Is there an onboarding process in place?

765. Are the Chatbots Strategy project team members located locally to the users/stakeholders?

766. How are stakeholders chosen and what roles might they have on a Chatbots Strategy project?

767. Is the performance of the supplier to be rated and documented?

768. Where are the verification requirements to be documented (eg purchase order, agreement etc)?

769. Does the Chatbots Strategy project have a formal Chatbots Strategy project Charter?

770. How accurate and complete is the information?

771. Have stakeholder accountabilities & responsibilities been clearly defined?

772. What specific resources will be required for implementation activities?

773. Who will be collecting information?

774. Is there a formal process for updating the Chatbots Strategy project baseline?

775. What preventative action can be taken to reduce the likelihood a risk will be realised?

776. Are written status reports provided on a designated frequent basis?

2.39 Change Management Plan: Chatbots Strategy

777. What are the responsibilities assigned to each role?

778. Does this change represent a completely new process for your organization, or a different application of an existing process?

779. Where will the funds come from?

780. Do the proposed users have access to the appropriate documentation?

781. What risks may occur upfront, during implementation and after implementation?

782. Has the training provider been established?

783. What are the current methods of sharing information and do there need to be new ones developed?

784. Why is the initiative is being undertaken - What are the business drivers?

785. What is the most positive interpretation it can receive?

786. Which relationships will change?

787. What are the specific target groups/audiences

that will be impacted by this change?

788. How will you deal with anger about the restricting of communications due to confidentiality considerations?

789. Identify the current level of skills and knowledge and behaviours of the group that will be impacted on. What prerequisite knowledge do corresponding groups need?

790. Readiness -what is a successful end state?

791. Who will be the change levers?

792. Do you need new systems?

793. What new behaviours are required?

794. What do you expect the target audience to do, say, think or feel as a result of this communication?

3.0 Executing Process Group: Chatbots Strategy

795. On which process should team members spend the most time?

796. What are the Chatbots Strategy project management deliverables of each process group?

797. Will new hardware or software be required for servers or client machines?

798. How does a Chatbots Strategy project life cycle differ from a product life cycle?

799. Who will provide training?

800. Does the Chatbots Strategy project team have the right skills?

801. What is the difference between using brainstorming and the Delphi technique for risk identification?

802. What type of people would you want on your team?

803. How well did the chosen processes fit the needs of the Chatbots Strategy project?

804. What is in place for ensuring adequate change control on Chatbots Strategy projects that involve outside contracts?

805. Could a new application negatively affect the current IT infrastructure?

806. What are the main parts of the scope statement?

807. Based on your Chatbots Strategy project communication management plan, what worked well?

808. Is the schedule for the set products being met?

809. What does it mean to take a systems view of a Chatbots Strategy project?

3.1 Team Member Status Report: Chatbots Strategy

810. How it is to be done?

811. What is to be done?

812. Does the product, good, or service already exist within your organization?

813. The problem with Reward & Recognition Programs is that the truly deserving people all too often get left out. How can you make it practical?

814. Do you have an Enterprise Chatbots Strategy project Management Office (EPMO)?

815. Are the attitudes of staff regarding Chatbots Strategy project work improving?

816. How much risk is involved?

817. When a teams productivity and success depend on collaboration and the efficient flow of information, what generally fails them?

818. Does every department have to have a Chatbots Strategy project Manager on staff?

819. How will resource planning be done?

820. Will the staff do training or is that done by a third party?

821. How does this product, good, or service meet the needs of the Chatbots Strategy project and your organization as a whole?

822. Does your organization have the means (staff, money, contract, etc.) to produce or to acquire the product, good, or service?

823. Are the products of your organizations Chatbots Strategy projects meeting customers objectives?

824. Are your organizations Chatbots Strategy projects more successful over time?

825. Why is it to be done?

826. What specific interest groups do you have in place?

827. Is there evidence that staff is taking a more professional approach toward management of your organizations Chatbots Strategy projects?

828. How can you make it practical?

3.2 Change Request: Chatbots Strategy

829. What must be taken into consideration when introducing change control programs?

830. How are changes requested (forms, method of communication)?

831. Are there requirements attributes that can discriminate between high and low reliability?

832. What is the change request log?

833. What can be filed?

834. Has a formal technical review been conducted to assess technical correctness?

835. Will this change conflict with other requirements changes (e.g., lead to conflicting operational scenarios)?

836. Why were your requested changes rejected or not made?

837. What mechanism is used to appraise others of changes that are made?

838. Why do you want to have a change control system?

839. Will the change use memory to the extent that

other functions will be not have sufficient memory to operate effectively?

840. What has an inspector to inspect and to check?

841. What are the basic mechanics of the Change Advisory Board (CAB)?

842. Since there are no change requests in your Chatbots Strategy project at this point, what must you have before you begin?

843. Describe how modifications, enhancements, defects and/or deficiencies shall be notified (e.g. Problem Reports, Change Requests etc) and managed. Detail warranty and/or maintenance periods?

844. Which requirements attributes affect the risk to reliability the most?

845. Who has responsibility for approving and ranking changes?

846. Will there be a change request form in use?

847. How does a team identify the discrete elements of a configuration?

848. Are you implementing itil processes?

3.3 Change Log: Chatbots Strategy

849. Is this a mandatory replacement?

850. When was the request submitted?

851. How does this change affect the timeline of the schedule?

852. How does this relate to the standards developed for specific business processes?

853. Is the change request open, closed or pending?

854. Does the suggested change request seem to represent a necessary enhancement to the product?

855. Will the Chatbots Strategy project fail if the change request is not executed?

856. Do the described changes impact on the integrity or security of the system?

857. Is the change backward compatible without limitations?

858. Is the change request within Chatbots Strategy project scope?

859. How does this change affect scope?

860. Who initiated the change request?

861. Is the submitted change a new change or a

modification of a previously approved change?

862. Should a more thorough impact analysis be conducted?

863. When was the request approved?

864. Is the requested change request a result of changes in other Chatbots Strategy project(s)?

3.4 Decision Log: Chatbots Strategy

865. Is everything working as expected?

866. How does an increasing emphasis on cost containment influence the strategies and tactics used?

867. Do strategies and tactics aimed at less than full control reduce the costs of management or simply shift the cost burden?

868. Does anything need to be adjusted?

869. What is the line where eDiscovery ends and document review begins?

870. Who is the decisionmaker?

871. It becomes critical to track and periodically revisit both operational effectiveness; Are you noticing all that you need to, and are you interpreting what you see effectively?

872. What alternatives/risks were considered?

873. What is your overall strategy for quality control / quality assurance procedures?

874. What eDiscovery problem or issue did your organization set out to fix or make better?

875. What was the rationale for the decision?

876. How does provision of information, both in terms of content and presentation, influence acceptance of alternative strategies?

877. How do you define success?

878. Linked to original objective?

879. Meeting purpose; why does this team meet?

880. Is your opponent open to a non-traditional workflow, or will it likely challenge anything you do?

881. What are the cost implications?

882. What is the average size of your matters in an applicable measurement?

883. At what point in time does loss become unacceptable?

884. How effective is maintaining the log at facilitating organizational learning?

3.5 Quality Audit: Chatbots Strategy

885. Are people allowed to contribute ideas?

886. How does your organization know that its information technology system is serving its needs as effectively and constructively as is appropriate?

887. How does your organization know that its system for staff performance planning and review is appropriately effective and constructive?

888. How does your organization know that its system for governing staff behaviour is appropriately effective and constructive?

889. Do the acceptance procedures and specifications include the criteria for acceptance/rejection, define the process to be used, and specify the measuring and test equipment that is to be used?

890. How well do you think your organization engages with the outside community?

891. How does your organization know that its planning processes are appropriately effective and constructive?

892. How does your organization know that it is appropriately effective and constructive in preparing its staff for organizational aspirations?

893. Are all records associated with the reconditioning of a device maintained for a minimum of two years

after the sale or disposal of the last device within a lot of merchandise?

894. Is progress against the intentions measurable?

895. Does the suppliers quality system have a written procedure for corrective action when a defect occurs?

896. How does your organization know that its management of its ethical responsibilities is appropriately effective and constructive?

897. Has a written procedure been established to identify devices during all stages of receipt, reconditioning, distribution and installation so that mix-ups are prevented?

898. How does your organization know that its relationships with other relevant organizations are appropriately effective and constructive?

899. Does the supplier use a formal quality system?

900. How does your organization know that the support for its staff is appropriately effective and constructive?

901. How does your organization know that its system for ensuring a positive organizational climate is appropriately effective and constructive?

902. How does your organization know that its system for ensuring that its training activities are appropriately resourced and support is appropriately effective and constructive?

903. Do prior clients have a positive opinion of your organization?

904. Are the intentions consistent with external obligations (such as applicable laws)?

3.6 Team Directory: Chatbots Strategy

905. How and in what format should information be presented?

906. Days from the time the issue is identified?

907. Do purchase specifications and configurations match requirements?

908. Who will report Chatbots Strategy project status to all stakeholders?

909. Timing: when do the effects of communication take place?

910. What needs to be communicated?

911. How will you accomplish and manage the objectives?

912. Who are the Team Members?

913. How do unidentified risks impact the outcome of the Chatbots Strategy project?

914. Process decisions: do job conditions warrant additional actions to collect job information and document on-site activity?

915. Where should the information be distributed?

916. Process decisions: are all start-up, turn over and close out requirements of the contract satisfied?

917. When does information need to be distributed?

918. Who should receive information (all stakeholders)?

919. Process decisions: are contractors adequately prosecuting the work?

920. How will the team handle changes?

921. Process decisions: how well was task order work performed?

922. Who will talk to the customer?

3.7 Team Operating Agreement: Chatbots Strategy

923. Do you begin with a question to engage everyone?

924. What is a Virtual Team?

925. Must your members collaborate successfully to complete Chatbots Strategy projects?

926. Is compensation based on team and individual performance?

927. Do you listen for voice tone and word choice to understand the meaning behind words?

928. Conflict resolution: how will disputes and other conflicts be mediated or resolved?

929. Do you ensure that all participants know how to use the required technology?

930. Do you upload presentation materials in advance and test the technology?

931. Did you delegate tasks such as taking meeting minutes, presenting a topic and soliciting input?

932. What resources can be provided for the team in terms of equipment, space, time for training, protected time and space for meetings, and travel allowances?

933. What administrative supports will be put in place to support the team and the teams supervisor?

934. Have you established procedures that team members can follow to work effectively together, such as a team operating agreement?

935. How does teaming fit in with overall organizational goals and meet organizational needs?

936. Do team members reside in more than two countries?

937. What are the safety issues/risks that need to be addressed and/or that the team needs to consider?

938. Do you call or email participants to ensure understanding, follow-through and commitment to the meeting outcomes?

939. What are the current caseload numbers in the unit?

940. Are team roles clearly defined and accepted?

941. What types of accommodations will be formulated and put in place for sustaining the team?

942. Why does your organization want to participate in teaming?

3.8 Team Performance Assessment: Chatbots Strategy

943. To what degree do all members feel responsible for all agreed-upon measures?

944. Is there a particular method of data analysis that you would recommend as a means of demonstrating that method variance is not of great concern for a given dataset?

945. To what degree are fresh input and perspectives systematically caught and added (for example, through information and analysis, new members, and senior sponsors)?

946. To what degree are the goals realistic?

947. Do friends perform better than acquaintances?

948. To what degree are the members clear on what they are individually responsible for and what they are jointly responsible for?

949. Where to from here?

950. To what degree are the skill areas critical to team performance present?

951. To what degree does the teams approach to its work allow for modification and improvement over time?

952. How does Chatbots Strategy project termination impact Chatbots Strategy project team members?

953. To what degree are the teams goals and objectives clear, simple, and measurable?

954. Do you promptly inform members about major developments that may affect them?

955. What is method variance?

956. To what degree can team members vigorously define the teams purpose in considerations with others who are not part of the functioning team?

957. Do you give group members authority to make at least some important decisions?

958. To what degree do team members articulate the teams work approach?

959. How hard did you try to make a good selection?

960. To what degree will the approach capitalize on and enhance the skills of all team members in a manner that takes into consideration other demands on members of the team?

961. To what degree are the relative importance and priority of the goals clear to all team members?

962. How do you keep key people outside the group informed about its accomplishments?

3.9 Team Member Performance Assessment: Chatbots Strategy

963. What is needed for effective data teams?

964. What were the challenges that resulted for training and assessment?

965. How are assessments designed, delivered, and otherwise used to maximize training?

966. How should adaptive assessments be implemented?

967. What are top priorities?

968. What innovations (if any) are developed to realize goals?

969. Does platform-specific assessment information contribute to training placement or tailoring of instruction (e.g. aptitude-treatment interaction)?

970. How do you start collaborating?

971. How do you work together to improve teaching and learning?

972. What are the staffs preferences for training on technology-based platforms?

973. What is a general description of the processes under performance measurement and assessment?

974. Does adaptive training work?

975. What are acceptable governance changes?

976. To what degree do team members understand one anothers roles and skills?

977. To what degree are the goals ambitious?

978. In what areas would you like to concentrate your knowledge and resources?

979. Which training platform formats (i.e., mobile, virtual, videogame-based) were implemented in your effort(s)?

980. How do you make use of research?

3.10 Issue Log: Chatbots Strategy

981. Which stakeholders can influence others?

982. What are the stakeholders interrelationships?

983. Do you often overlook a key stakeholder or stakeholder group?

984. In classifying stakeholders, which approach to do so are you using?

985. What effort will a change need?

986. Is access to the Issue Log controlled?

987. Do you prepare stakeholder engagement plans?

988. Can an impact cause deviation beyond team, stage or Chatbots Strategy project tolerances?

989. Are you constantly rushing from meeting to meeting?

990. Are there common objectives between the team and the stakeholder?

991. Can you think of other people who might have concerns or interests?

992. What is a change?

993. Why do you manage communications?

994. How much time does it take to do it?

995. Is it a change in scope?

996. Are the stakeholders getting the information they need, are they consulted, are concerns addressed?

4.0 Monitoring and Controlling Process Group: Chatbots Strategy

997. Are the services being delivered?

998. Were escalated issues resolved promptly?

999. Who needs to be engaged upfront to ensure use of results?

1000. Are there areas that need improvement?

1001. How were collaborations developed, and how are they sustained?

1002. How can you monitor progress?

1003. Where is the Risk in the Chatbots Strategy project?

1004. When will the Chatbots Strategy project be done?

1005. How is agile program management done?

1006. How can you make your needs known?

1007. What input will you be required to provide the Chatbots Strategy project team?

1008. How well did the chosen processes produce the expected results?

1009. Is there undesirable impact on staff or resources?

1010. What areas were overlooked on this Chatbots Strategy project?

1011. How do you monitor progress?

1012. Mitigate. what will you do to minimize the impact should a risk event occur?

1013. Use: how will they use the information?

1014. Did the Chatbots Strategy project team have the right skills?

1015. How is agile Chatbots Strategy project management done?

1016. Do the products created live up to the necessary quality?

4.1 Project Performance Report: Chatbots Strategy

1017. To what degree does the task meet individual needs?

1018. To what degree do team members frequently explore the teams purpose and its implications?

1019. To what degree will the team adopt a concrete, clearly understood, and agreed-upon approach that will result in achievement of the teams goals?

1020. To what degree will the team ensure that all members equitably share the work essential to the success of the team?

1021. To what degree does the information network communicate information relevant to the task?

1022. To what degree do the relationships of the informal organization motivate taskrelevant behavior and facilitate task completion?

1023. To what degree can the team ensure that all members are individually and jointly accountable for the teams purpose, goals, approach, and work-products?

1024. What is the degree to which rules govern information exchange between groups?

1025. To what degree are the tasks requirements

reflected in the flow and storage of information?

1026. To what degree is the information network consistent with the structure of the formal organization?

1027. To what degree will new and supplemental skills be introduced as the need is recognized?

1028. To what degree will team members, individually and collectively, commit time to help themselves and others learn and develop skills?

1029. To what degree do individual skills and abilities match task demands?

1030. How can Chatbots Strategy project sustainability be maintained?

1031. To what degree does the team possess adequate membership to achieve its ends?

1032. To what degree is the team cognizant of small wins to be celebrated along the way?

1033. How will procurement be coordinated with other Chatbots Strategy project aspects, such as scheduling and performance reporting?

4.2 Variance Analysis: Chatbots Strategy

1034. Do the rates and prices remain constant throughout the year?

1035. Is work progressively subdivided into detailed work packages as requirements are defined?

1036. What causes selling price variance?

1037. Are records maintained to show how undistributed budgets are controlled?

1038. Is budgeted cost for work performed calculated in a manner consistent with the way work is planned?

1039. Is the entire contract planned in time-phased control accounts to the extent practicable?

1040. What is the actual cost of work performed?

1041. What does a favorable labor efficiency variance mean?

1042. Did a new competitor enter the market?

1043. What are the actual costs to date?

1044. Are data elements reconcilable between internal summary reports and reports forwarded to the stakeholders?

1045. What is exceptional?

1046. Are records maintained to show how management reserves are used?

1047. Are management actions taken to reduce indirect costs when there are significant adverse variances?

1048. Who are responsible for the establishment of budgets and assignment of resources for overhead performance?

1049. Are all cwbs elements specified for external reporting?

1050. Can process improvements lead to unfavorable variances?

1051. Are all elements of indirect expense identified to overhead cost budgets of Chatbots Strategy projections?

1052. Are authorized changes being incorporated in a timely manner?

4.3 Earned Value Status: Chatbots Strategy

1053. Where is evidence-based earned value in your organization reported?

1054. Earned value can be used in almost any Chatbots Strategy project situation and in almost any Chatbots Strategy project environment. it may be used on large Chatbots Strategy projects, medium sized Chatbots Strategy projects, tiny Chatbots Strategy projects (in cut-down form), complex and simple Chatbots Strategy projects and in any market sector. some people, of course, know all about earned value, they have used it for years - but perhaps not as effectively as they could have?

1055. Where are your problem areas?

1056. How much is it going to cost by the finish?

1057. What is the unit of forecast value?

1058. When is it going to finish?

1059. How does this compare with other Chatbots Strategy projects?

1060. If earned value management (EVM) is so good in determining the true status of a Chatbots Strategy project and Chatbots Strategy project its completion, why is it that hardly any one uses it in information systems related Chatbots Strategy projects?

1061. Verification is a process of ensuring that the developed system satisfies the stakeholders agreements and specifications; Are you building the product right? What do you verify?

1062. Are you hitting your Chatbots Strategy projects targets?

1063. Validation is a process of ensuring that the developed system will actually achieve the stakeholders desired outcomes; Are you building the right product? What do you validate?

4.4 Risk Audit: Chatbots Strategy

1064. Do you have written and signed agreements/ contracts in place for each paid staff member?

1065. Do you have proper induction processes for all new paid staff and volunteers who have a specific role and responsibility?

1066. Does your organization have an up-to-date constitution?

1067. Do you have a mechanism for managing change?

1068. Do you ensure the recommended rules of play and protocols are followed for your activity?

1069. Do you have position descriptions for all office bearers/staff?

1070. Does your organization meet the terms of any contracts with which it is involved?

1071. How do you prioritize risks?

1072. Do you have an emergency plan?

1073. Is risk an management agenda item?

1074. Are audit program plans risk-adjusted?

1075. What are the outcomes you are looking for?

1076. Improving fraud detection: do auditors react to abnormal inconsistencies between financial and non-financial measures?

1077. Is the customer willing to participate in reviews?

1078. What are risks and how do you manage them?

1079. Does your organization have a social media policy and procedure?

1080. Is there a screening process that will ensure all participants have the fitness and skills required to safely participate?

1081. Can analytical tests provide evidence that is as strong as evidence from traditional substantive tests?

1082. Do you have a procedure for dealing with complaints?

4.5 Contractor Status Report: Chatbots Strategy

1083. How is risk transferred?

1084. What was the overall budget or estimated cost?

1085. What was the actual budget or estimated cost for your organizations services?

1086. Who can list a Chatbots Strategy project as organization experience, your organization or a previous employee of your organization?

1087. What was the final actual cost?

1088. Describe how often regular updates are made to the proposed solution. Are corresponding regular updates included in the standard maintenance plan?

1089. What process manages the contracts?

1090. What was the budget or estimated cost for your organizations services?

1091. If applicable; describe your standard schedule for new software version releases. Are new software version releases included in the standard maintenance plan?

1092. What are the minimum and optimal bandwidth requirements for the proposed solution?

1093. How does the proposed individual meet each requirement?

1094. What is the average response time for answering a support call?

1095. Are there contractual transfer concerns?

1096. How long have you been using the services?

4.6 Formal Acceptance: Chatbots Strategy

1097. Was the client satisfied with the Chatbots Strategy project results?

1098. Does it do what client said it would?

1099. What is the Acceptance Management Process?

1100. Who would use it?

1101. Do you perform formal acceptance or burn-in tests?

1102. Do you buy pre-configured systems or build your own configuration?

1103. General estimate of the costs and times to complete the Chatbots Strategy project?

1104. What are the requirements against which to test, Who will execute?

1105. What function(s) does it fill or meet?

1106. Was the Chatbots Strategy project goal achieved?

1107. Do you buy-in installation services?

1108. Have all comments been addressed?

1109. What can you do better next time?

1110. What features, practices, and processes proved to be strengths or weaknesses?

1111. Did the Chatbots Strategy project achieve its MOV?

1112. Was the sponsor/customer satisfied?

1113. Is formal acceptance of the Chatbots Strategy project product documented and distributed?

1114. How does your team plan to obtain formal acceptance on your Chatbots Strategy project?

1115. Who supplies data?

1116. What lessons were learned about your Chatbots Strategy project management methodology?

5.0 Closing Process Group: Chatbots Strategy

1117. What was learned?

1118. What is the amount of funding and what Chatbots Strategy project phases are funded?

1119. Can the lesson learned be replicated?

1120. Is this an updated Chatbots Strategy project Proposal Document?

1121. Is this a follow-on to a previous Chatbots Strategy project?

1122. What areas were overlooked on this Chatbots Strategy project?

1123. What will you do to minimize the impact should a risk event occur?

1124. What will you do?

1125. What is an Encumbrance?

1126. What business situation is being addressed?

1127. How will you know you did it?

1128. Did the delivered product meet the specified requirements and goals of the Chatbots Strategy project?

1129. How well did the chosen processes fit the needs of the Chatbots Strategy project?

1130. Will the Chatbots Strategy project deliverable(s) replace a current asset or group of assets?

5.1 Procurement Audit: Chatbots Strategy

1131. Do the internal control systems function appropriate?

1132. Does an appropriately qualified official check the quality of performance against the contract terms?

1133. Is data securely stored?

1134. Were any additional works or deliveries admissible, without recourse to a new procurement procedure?

1135. Are the official minutes written in a clear and concise manner?

1136. Are cases of double payment duly prevented and corrected?

1137. Has a deputy treasurer been appointed to sign checks when the treasurer is unable to perform that duty?

1138. Were additional deliveries a partial replacement for normal supplies or installations or an extension of existing supplies or installations?

1139. Did the chosen procedure ensure competition and transparency?

1140. Are internal control mechanisms performed before payments?

1141. Is there any objection?

1142. Does the procurement unit have sound commercial awareness and knowledge of suppliers and the market?

1143. Does the strategy ensure that the best supplier is chosen considering: price, quality, service, dependable operation, internal operation costs, life time operation costs and codes of ethic?

1144. How do you confirm whether the contracted organization supplied the goods or executed the work as per the quality, quantity and price indicated in the contract agreement/ supply order?

1145. What are the required standards of quality assurance or environmental management?

1146. Was suitability of candidates accurately assessed?

1147. Does the strategy ensure that needs are met, and not exceeded?

1148. Are all mutilated and voided checks retained for proper accounting of pre-numbered checks?

1149. Did your organization calculate the contract value accurately?

1150. Is the strategy implemented across the entire organization?

5.2 Contract Close-Out: Chatbots Strategy

1151. Have all contract records been included in the Chatbots Strategy project archives?

1152. Change in knowledge?

1153. Was the contract type appropriate?

1154. Change in circumstances?

1155. Change in attitude or behavior?

1156. How/when used ?

1157. Are the signers the authorized officials?

1158. Has each contract been audited to verify acceptance and delivery?

1159. How does it work?

1160. Was the contract sufficiently clear so as not to result in numerous disputes and misunderstandings?

1161. Why Outsource?

1162. Have all contracts been closed?

1163. How is the contracting office notified of the automatic contract close-out?

1164. Have all acceptance criteria been met prior to final payment to contractors?

1165. Was the contract complete without requiring numerous changes and revisions?

1166. Parties: who is involved?

1167. What is capture management?

1168. What happens to the recipient of services?

1169. Parties: Authorized?

1170. Have all contracts been completed?

5.3 Project or Phase Close-Out: Chatbots Strategy

1171. What stakeholder group needs, expectations, and interests are being met by the Chatbots Strategy project?

1172. Planned completion date?

1173. What are they?

1174. Which changes might a stakeholder be required to make as a result of the Chatbots Strategy project?

1175. What is this stakeholder expecting?

1176. Were cost budgets met?

1177. If you were the Chatbots Strategy project sponsor, how would you determine which Chatbots Strategy project team(s) and/or individuals deserve recognition?

1178. What were the goals and objectives of the communications strategy for the Chatbots Strategy project?

1179. Is there a clear cause and effect between the activity and the lesson learned?

1180. What information is each stakeholder group interested in?

1181. What advantages do the an individual interview have over a group meeting, and vice-versa?

1182. Who controlled the resources for the Chatbots Strategy project?

1183. What hierarchical authority does the stakeholder have in your organization?

1184. What can you do better next time, and what specific actions can you take to improve?

1185. Is the lesson significant, valid, and applicable?

1186. What could have been improved?

1187. Does the lesson describe a function that would be done differently the next time?

1188. What is a Risk?

1189. What is the information level of detail required for each stakeholder?

1190. Was the schedule met?

5.4 Lessons Learned: Chatbots Strategy

1191. What solutions or recommendations can you offer that would have improved some aspect of the Chatbots Strategy project?

1192. How effective was the quality assurance process?

1193. What is (are) the indicator(s) of success?

1194. How does the budget cycle affect the case?

1195. What is the value of the deliverable?

1196. What are the expectations of the individuals?

1197. Are you in full regulatory compliance?

1198. How effective was the acceptance management process?

1199. Was there a Chatbots Strategy project Definition document. Was there a Chatbots Strategy project Plan. Were they used during the Chatbots Strategy project?

1200. How effective was the documentation that you received with the Chatbots Strategy project product/service?

1201. Under what legal authority did your

organization head and program manager direct your organization and Chatbots Strategy project?

1202. How much flexibility is there in the funding (e.g., what authorities does the program manager have to change to the specifics of the funding within the overall funding ceiling)?

1203. What were the success factors?

1204. Are there any hidden conflicts of interest?

1205. What worked well or did not work well, either for this Chatbots Strategy project or for the Chatbots Strategy project team?

1206. How much time is required for the task?

1207. How useful do individuals find communications?

1208. What regulatory regime controlled how your organization head and program manager directed your organization and Chatbots Strategy project?

1209. Do you conduct the engineering tests?

Index

addition 112
additional 32, 38, 59, 61-62, 64, 157, 169, 179, 228, 254
additions 98
address 21, 76, 130, 136, 193
addressed 166, 195, 197, 231, 237, 250, 252
addressing 35, 121
adequate 30, 150, 155, 170, 175, 211, 215, 241
adequately 32, 136, 229
adhered 154
adjust 91, 98
adjusted 99, 223
admissible 254
advance 200, 209, 230
advantage 71, 121, 185
advantages 109, 259
adverse 243
Advisory 220
affect 64, 113, 124, 129, 133, 140, 145, 148, 181, 203, 216, 220-221, 233, 260
affected 133, 155
affecting 11, 24, 63, 135
affects 169
afford 198-199
affordable 75
against 33, 93, 100, 139, 154, 182-183, 226, 250, 254
agencies 201
agenda 246
agendas 108
aggregate 46
agreed 141, 207
agreement 5, 175, 211, 230-231, 255
agreements 64, 77, 245-246
agrees 126, 188
aiming 122
alerting 141
alerts 96
aligned 25
aligns 175
alleged 1
alliance 82
allocate 120, 178
allocated 49, 114
allocating 190

briefed 38
brings 40
broken 66
broker 156
budget   97, 99, 123, 129, 137, 154-155, 158, 171, 173, 175-178, 181, 203, 248, 260
budgeted   56, 154, 189, 242
budgeting   155
budgets   16, 154-155, 189-190, 242-243, 258
building   17, 93, 245
burden 223
burn-in 250
business   1, 7, 9, 17, 19, 30, 43, 52, 63, 83, 91, 106-107, 109, 111-112, 114-116, 122, 128, 143, 175, 185, 189, 197, 213, 221, 252
buy-in 116, 250
calculate   170, 255
calculated   242
called 129
candidates   255
cannot 154, 173
capability   24, 211
capable   7, 32, 190
capacities   119
capacity   17, 24, 76, 208
capital 110
capitalize   67, 233
capture   50, 93, 257
captured   48, 63, 86, 126, 140, 143, 175, 193-194, 211
capturing   177
career 145
careers   106
carried 65, 193, 205
caseload   231
categories   197
category   33, 155
caught 232
caused   1, 53
causes 47, 50, 54, 58, 61, 69-70, 96, 137, 205, 242
causing   24
ceiling 261
celebrate   75
celebrated   241
center 56

hitting 245
honest 107
humans   7
hypotheses   58
identified   1, 17, 20, 24, 32, 39, 60-61, 63, 68, 78, 84, 128,
147-148, 154-157, 175, 185, 189, 191, 194, 199-200, 202-203, 205,
211, 228, 243
identifier   130
identifies   204
identify9-10, 17-18, 59, 62, 82, 133, 147, 151, 154, 162, 179, 210,
214, 220, 226
ignore 18
ignoring   105
images143-144
imbedded   98
impact4, 31, 43-45, 49, 52, 55, 80, 104, 128, 199-201, 203, 221-
222, 228, 233, 236, 239, 252
impacted   46, 148, 214
impacting   173
impacts   49, 172
implement   17, 52, 61, 90
implicit 110
importance   233
important   18, 20, 65-66, 107, 112, 114, 119, 121, 133-135,
169-170, 209, 233
improve   2, 9, 70, 74-76, 78-83, 85, 88, 134, 167, 177, 184,
234, 259
improved   76, 78, 84, 88, 95, 136, 259-260
improves   129
improving   65, 75, 217, 247
incentives   98
include   19, 81, 158, 170, 175, 207, 225
included   2, 7, 19, 53, 143, 148, 155-156, 179, 248, 256
INCLUDES   9
including   24, 29, 38-39, 51, 57, 63, 92-93, 97
increase   83, 107
increased   114, 192
increasing   223
incurred   50
in-depth   8, 10
indicate   69, 93, 109
indicated   96, 255
indicator   260

manager 7, 9, 19, 30, 33, 112, 141, 148, 184, 217, 261
managers 2, 127-128, 140, 203, 208
manages 76, 80, 131, 248
managing 2, 82, 127, 132, 246
Mandated 203
mandatory 221
manner 15, 76, 150, 190, 193, 233, 242-243, 254
manpower 155
Mapping 81
market 26, 162, 197, 242, 244, 255
marketable 197
marketer 7
marketing 144
markets 21
Master 173
material 155, 162
materials 1, 230
matrices 145
Matrix 2-4, 133, 145, 189, 203
matter 36, 56
matters 224
maximize 234
maximizing 115
maximum 128
meaning 230
meaningful 53, 107
measurable 33, 37, 178, 226, 233
measure 2, 9, 17, 20, 28, 36, 43-45, 47, 50-51, 54, 63, 74, 78, 81-83, 88, 92, 95, 99, 133, 179-181, 183-184, 186, 204
measured 17, 44, 47, 51, 53, 56-57, 82, 92, 100, 185
measures 46, 52, 54-57, 60, 63, 65-66, 77, 91, 93, 185, 232, 247
measuring 90, 225
mechanical 1
mechanics 220
mechanism 219, 246
mechanisms 255
mediated 230
medium 244
meeting 30, 41, 97, 182, 192, 194, 218, 224, 230-231, 236, 259
meetings 28, 31, 34, 40, 142, 230
megatrends 111

primary   46, 130, 167
priorities   46-47, 51, 53, 55, 234
prioritize   203, 246
priority 44, 52, 233
privacy   32, 185
problem   15-16, 18-21, 23-24, 27, 31, 37-38, 51, 53, 64, 71,
143, 217, 220, 223, 244
problems   15, 18, 21-22, 24, 75, 77, 86, 96, 119, 209
procedure   154, 183, 226, 247, 254
procedures   9, 82, 91-92, 99-100, 150, 156, 166, 169, 174-176,
184, 187, 194, 223, 225, 231
process   1-7, 9, 28, 30-31, 34, 36-38, 56, 59-63, 65-68, 71-
72, 76, 83, 90-95, 97-100, 128-129, 135, 141-142, 144-148, 150-
151, 155-157, 166, 169, 171, 181, 183, 187-188, 191, 197, 200, 204,
210-213, 215, 225, 228-229, 238, 243, 245, 247-248, 250, 252, 260
processes   43, 46, 59-65, 67-68, 70-71, 91-92, 98, 129, 133,
136, 139, 154, 157, 183-184, 187, 199, 215, 220-221, 225, 234, 238,
246, 251, 253
procuring   155
produce   62, 166, 218, 238
produced   67, 85
produces   161
producing   145, 147
product   1, 65-66, 109, 111, 139, 141, 148, 162, 181-182,
197, 202, 205, 215, 217-218, 221, 245, 251-252, 260
production   40, 74, 114
products   1, 21-22, 45, 119, 135-136, 142, 145, 156, 182, 185,
216, 218, 239
profit   186
program   22, 46, 69, 99, 129, 136, 197, 199, 238, 246, 261
programs   217, 219
progress   38, 53, 88, 97, 103-105, 136, 151, 154, 175, 179,
187-188, 226, 238-239
prohibited   154
project 2-8, 17-18, 24, 41, 50, 62, 70, 77, 94, 98-100, 105, 108-110,
112, 118, 121, 125, 127-142, 145, 147-148, 151-154, 156-158, 160-
165, 167-171, 173-179, 181-182, 184, 190-195, 197-204, 207-208,
211-212, 215-218, 220-222, 228, 233, 236, 238-241, 244, 248, 250-
253, 256, 258-261
projection   65, 202
projects   2, 53, 124, 127, 129, 134-135, 140, 145, 150, 152,
169-170, 173, 181, 192, 201, 204, 208, 215, 218, 230, 244-245
promised   126

reports 45, 91, 132, 138, 141, 157, 212, 220, 242
repository   157, 176, 193
represent   82, 181, 213, 221
reproduced   1
reputation   120
request   5, 70-71, 141, 181, 219-222
requested   1, 81, 210, 219, 222
requests   210, 220
require 41, 50, 67, 72, 91, 101, 130, 166, 201
required   15, 22, 29, 33-34, 36, 40, 49, 55, 69, 71, 77, 85-86,
91, 128-129, 136, 139, 143, 150, 158-159, 185, 188, 194, 212, 214-
215, 230, 238, 247, 255, 258-259, 261
requiring   132, 257
research   26, 109, 118, 162, 235
Reserve   177
reserved   1
reserves   193, 243
reside 80, 157, 231
resolution   63, 230
resolve 15, 19, 23, 160
resolved   173, 197, 230, 238
resource   3-4, 124, 155, 160, 166-167, 193, 207, 217
resourced   226
resources   2, 7, 16-17, 19, 21, 27, 30, 32, 61, 85, 91, 97, 114-
115, 120, 124, 128-129, 140, 157, 159-160, 167-168, 171, 173, 179,
181, 208, 211-212, 230, 235, 239, 243, 259
respect   1
respond   136, 189
responded   11
response   22, 26, 93, 96, 98, 169, 249
responses   80, 107, 210
responsive   179
result   61, 82, 85, 148, 178-179, 185, 214, 222, 240, 256, 258
resulted   100, 234
resulting   70
results 8, 29, 34, 51, 65, 74-75, 79-81, 83, 85, 87, 92-93, 128, 135-
136, 140, 173, 179, 188, 201, 238, 250
Retain 103
retained   255
retention   45
return 85, 119, 165, 187
returns 186
revenue   18, 49

sector 244
securely   116, 254
securing   50, 125
security   17, 64, 78, 100-101, 132, 150-151, 221
seemed   170
segmented   32
segments   41, 124
select 59, 97
selected   84, 179-180, 201
selecting   62, 117, 137
selection   5, 209, 233
seller 208
sellers 1
selling 119, 162, 242
senior 93, 119, 121, 232
sensitive   55
sequencing   121, 169
series 10
servers 215
service 1-2, 7, 78-79, 82, 91, 109, 148, 162, 181, 197, 210, 217-218,
255, 260
services   1, 41, 45, 51, 54, 113, 119, 124, 133, 238, 248-250,
257
serving 225
session 158
setbacks   61, 71
setting 117, 122
several 67, 139
severely   66
shared 98, 179
sharing 84, 96, 129, 183, 213
shifts 19
shortest   170
should 7, 19-21, 23, 30, 36, 38, 45-46, 50, 59, 65-66, 71, 83-85, 92,
94, 112, 116, 120-122, 128-129, 132, 136-137, 142, 148, 151, 158,
160, 167, 171, 174, 178, 188, 192, 197, 199-200, 202-204, 209-210,
215, 222, 228-229, 234, 239, 252
signature   108
signatures   166
signed 147, 246
signers 256
similar 37, 41, 65, 72, 79, 158, 176
simple 112, 233, 244

simply 8, 223
single 111
single-use   7
situation   22, 43, 200, 244, 252
situations   98
skills   21, 24, 64, 107, 112, 123, 128, 163, 193, 199, 214-215, 233, 235, 239, 241, 247
smaller 135
smallest   18, 85
social 247
societal   110
software   22, 140-142, 169, 177, 193, 198, 203-204, 215, 248
solicit 32
soliciting   230
solution   63, 71, 74-75, 79-80, 84-85, 87, 90, 147, 206, 248
solutions   50, 77-78, 81-82, 92, 260
solved 20
Someone   7
something   126, 137, 151
Sometimes   50
source 5, 110, 118, 209
sources   41, 61, 72, 201
special 32, 92, 210
specific   8, 16, 33, 37, 39, 140-141, 150, 160-161, 163, 165-166, 176, 191, 193, 203, 212-213, 218, 221, 246, 259
specifics   261
specified   115, 154, 189, 243, 252
specify 225
Speech   144
spoken 106
sponsor   20, 131, 147, 251, 258
sponsored   35
sponsors   25, 232
spread 93, 99
stability 148
staffed 32
staffing 24, 98
staffs   234
stages 194, 226
stakes 133
standard   7, 91, 100, 166, 248
standards   1, 9-10, 91, 94-96, 98, 150, 156, 183, 194, 209, 221, 255

started 8
starting 9, 135
start-up   228
stated 117, 123, 157, 185, 189, 192
statement   3, 10, 75, 86, 147-148, 178, 181, 216
statements   11, 26, 37-38, 42, 57, 64, 73, 89, 102, 126, 141, 170
status 5-6, 64, 140, 148, 175, 197, 208, 212, 217, 228, 244, 248
Steering   176
stopper   143
storage   241
stored 254
stories 39
strategic   47, 86, 97, 130, 175
strategies   87, 118, 136, 197, 208, 223-224
Strategy   1-6, 8-13, 15-26, 28-90, 92-143, 145, 147-148, 150-
154, 156-158, 160-171, 173-179, 181-185, 187, 189-195, 197-205,
207-213, 215-223, 225, 228, 230, 232-234, 236, 238-246, 248, 250-
256, 258-261
Stream 81
strengths   151, 163, 251
stretch 122
strict   71
strive   122
strong   247
Strongly   10, 15, 27, 43, 58, 74, 90, 103
structure   3, 49, 77, 108, 112, 147-148, 152-153, 167, 209,
241
structured   123, 139
structures   136
stubborn   104
stupid 106
subdivided   242
subject 8-9, 36
Subjective   141, 186
subjects   69
submitted   221
subsequent   157
subset 18
succeed   50, 104
success   20, 28, 34-35, 38, 40, 44, 54, 57, 78, 82, 86, 100,
109, 116-117, 119, 123, 125, 128, 130, 164, 178, 217, 224, 240,
260-261
successes   107

Made in the USA
Columbia, SC
09 June 2021